Jerry Coker
The Teaching of Jazz

The Teaching of Jazz

by

Jerry Coker

ADVANCE MUSIC

"On Learning Music" by Howard M. Roberts is reprinted by permission of

"Afterword" from "The Jazz Idiom" by Jerry Coker (© 1975) is reprinted by permission of

the publisher, Prentice Hall, Inc., Englewood Cliffs, New Jersey.

Published by ADVANCE MUSIC

Rottenburg N.

ISBN 3-89221-028-4

(Hardcover Edition)

ISBN 3-89221-022-5

(Softcover Edition)

This book is dedicated, with love, to Elbert "Junie" Ferrell, saxophonist/improviser/arranger/teacher, dear friend, and the person who nutured my every musical need when I needed it most.

Table of Contents

Preface

I truly love jazz music, and I have felt that way all my life. I was blessed with parents and an older brother who were jazz musicians (my brother Jack still is), and who guided me musically and personally in my quest for a life in that music. Their living examples; their professional acquaintances and colleagues; their record-listening to great collections; and their care and feeding of my ears, mind and spirit, caused my discovery of jazz to be as natural as breath itself. The decision to make the music my life was my own doing, but without their example, I'm not sure that I would have received the full exposure to jazz needed to reach the point of having a choice presented to me. After all, by the time I was old enough to study music (1940), the enormously popular swing era of jazz was waning, to be replaced by the complex, esoteric style of bebop*, a style of jazz that was not likely to become a part of my environment without help from those around me. My grade school, junior high and high school, even the university I attended certainly did not expose me to jazz (though many of my fellow students at the university were playing jazz, there were no courses or much of any other use of that music). Although I was given

* an innovative, genius level art form which should have marked the transition of listening environment from night club to concert stage, just as virtuosity in classical music deserved a larger, formal, and respectful audience moving from salon or palace dining room to opera and concert halls.

the opportunity to study piano privately and placed in the school band on clarinet before I was a teenager, John Thompson piano methods and concert band music were devoid of jazz. Television wasn't in popular use yet, tape recorders hadn't been invented, jazz records were scarce, and so radio was about the only common medium for hearing jazz (and compared to today's programming of rock music, jazz was relatively scarce on radio as well). But radio enabled me to hear my father soloing with various bands, or an occasional live broadcast of Benny Goodman or Woody Herman; and there was *one* late night jazz disc jockey in nearby Chicago named Dave Garroway (later the originator of NBC's Today Show) who played good jazz recordings and offered insightful commentary. By the time of my llth birthday, I *knew* I wanted to be a jazz musician, and started playing professionally six months later. At this point, my parents decided to send me to a great jazz saxophonist-teacher, Junie Ferrell, luring me there by telling me that he could play the entire Coleman Hawkins solo on "Body and Soul" (recorded in 1939 and very much in my attention at the time) from memory. Junie became my jazz guru, teaching me saxophone, improvisation, saxophone section playing, composition, and arranging, over the next seven years. He was an excellent role model, too. He loved jazz, played beautifully, was a tasteful arranger, and an extremely dedicated teacher. When the time came, he sent me to another teacher, Santy Runyon, for the next stage in my development.

How different it is today for the would-be student of jazz music! Though still far from the ideal, the world's awareness of jazz as an art form has been permanently established. Recordings abound in such numbers, made and consumed all over the globe, that it has become impossible for a single individual to hear them all. Jazz ensembles, some astoundingly good, exist in many public school systems, and publishers of compositions and arrangements for those ensembles are numerous. There are many books on jazz, some for each level of ability and understanding. At this writing, there are 540 jazz tunes and about

100 exercise tracks on accompaniment recordings (play-a-longs) with which jazz students can practice. Most major cities have radio stations that play jazz at certain hours. Public television stations program jazz performances. Grants are available for studying and creating jazz music. There are instructional video tapes in jazz. Festivals, lectures, clinics, workshops, summer camps, and visiting artists in jazz are available daily somewhere in the world. Most universities today offer college credit for at least one jazz course. A jazz history course in a large university is likely to have 50-250 students enrolled for the course. Degree programs in jazz are offered in about 100 universities at present, and more new programs are begun each year. Approximately 20 universities offer jazz study at the Master of Music degree level. Membership in the National Association of Jazz Educators has increased, numbering in the thousands. That organization has annual conventions of impressive size and activity, and publishes its own bimonthly journal.

At the time of my growing up, no one could have foreseen that there would someday be an occupational field of jazz education, with its attendant degree programs, books, methods, and its large number of participants; students, teachers, and businessmen (publishers, agents, organizers, etc.). I presumed, even as my students do today, that my love and effort in studying jazz would perhaps reward me with a life in professional music, as a *performer* and/or a composer/arranger. It was a hard blow, then, to discover that although I loved the music, I didn't like the life, at least not altogether. Traveling and living out of a suitcase can get old in a hurry. The business of music (money, agents, managers, clubowners, etc.) wasn't my "bag". The thought of raising a family on the road seemed impossible. The road life left little or no time for practicing, jamming, rehearsing, reading, composing, and listening to other groups and records. Even good health was difficult to maintain. I quickly learned that earning an acceptable income in jazz involved going on the road to promote my records in order to achieve and keep up the notoriety or fame needed for bookings. It seemed like the end of the world, at least the world I was interested in. I tried staying in one large city, hoping to be a good local professional who wouldn't have to travel, but very few cities have jazz clubs that can stay afloat, so that was disappointing. I knew I still wanted to stay close to my beloved jazz... but how?

Like my old teacher, Junie Ferrell, I began teaching privately, both because I wanted supplementary income and because I had always felt an obligation to assist younger versions of myself in their efforts to learn jazz. Perhaps due to the fact that I was obsessively absorbed in teaching them, which also entailed devising methods and materials needed to feed their voracious appetites to learn, I was not aware of the larger picture; that is, that they were developing quickly, I was enjoying the process of working with them, and I was becoming a happier person. My wife, Patty, who had encouraged my first teaching efforts a few years prior to that, noticed the welcome change in my attitude and suggested that perhaps I'd like to go back to school, complete my degrees, and enter a life of teaching at the university level. It appealed to me greatly, though neither of us could anticipate that it would lead to teaching *jazz* at the college level. In 1958, Bill Lee, then Chairman of the Music Department at Sam Houston State University, offered me my first teaching position, and with true foresight, made it a position designed for starting jazz courses. A few years later, Dr. Lee became Dean of the Miami School of Music, and again offered me a challenge. This time my assignment was to create a jazz degree program from scratch. In 1966, this was new territory. He gave me the freedom and responsibility to invent courses, decide their logical sequence, design the curriculum, and teach everything in that curriculum until such time that the number of jazz majors made it possible to expand the faculty and obtain clerical help. It was very hard and lonely work, but it was a dream come true. It gave me the rare opportunity to pioneer the development of jazz education, without having to yield to preconceived ideas and policies (there weren't any!) or even the opinions of others who might not share my abiding love for the music. I *had* the support of a dean who did share my love of the music, and in reviewing the program at the end of each year, I sought feedback from him, from the faculty, graduate assistants, and students. The program was revised many times, until it was as close to perfection as could be achieved. All that remained was to learn to teach that curriculum to the best of our ability. If the resulting system were truly valid, that would become obvious if alumni became consistently successful. To our great joy, many alumni have made outstanding careers in jazz music.

If all of this seems more like a biography, testimony, and history than a preface, it is because my thirty years of teaching jazz add up to experience which might be repeated and shared, with some variations, by the readers of this book. All students of jazz should spend time in professional music, acquire experiences and successes, and strive to be the best performers possible with their developed God-given talents, even if they hope someday to become teachers. And when and if they do become teachers, they should still strive to become better performers. The best teachers are not failures and drop-outs from the professional world. They will be able to demonstrate what they preach to their students, remain active as performers, and devote great quantities of time and energy to realizing their fullest potential as jazz educators as well. It is not uncommon for one of my students, who primarily entered the jazz program here at the University of Tennessee to prepare for the professional life, to come to me and say that the goal is no longer strictly performance, because, after watching me teach, a career as an educator has become appealing. A life of service is *obviously* satisfying. I of course urge them, both for their sake and for their future students', to spend at least some time in the professional world. After all, performance is the name of the game. I also understand the attraction to the life of a jazz educator.

Jazz education *could* become everything you've ever wanted...

creativity, expression, learning, security, excitement, and the joy of watching others discover jazz. Perhaps it's not for everyone, but I for one, wouldn't trade places with anyone. I am in service to my fellow man, yet I will continue to express myself through my horn for as long as I'm still breathing.

1

Rationale

Any great idea that is worthy of being presented, instigated, developed, and brought to sucessful fruition is worthy of, and can withstand, careful scrutiny and consideration beforehand. Short-sightedness and hasty action must be avoided. The idea has to survive the tests of definition, philosophy, function, practical application, and expected results. And our part in that idea requires that we understand how the idea relates to those tests, and that our motivations for becoming involved with the idea are as worthy as the idea itself. In the case of this study, the "idea" is jazz education. It is not enough that you have taken someone else's word for it, or that the idea has succeeded elsewhere and therefore must be a valid undertaking. *You* need to carefully contemplate the rationale for the idea and *your* part in that idea. Although many facets of the idea will be presented to you throughout this book, you have a responsibility to continually add to, revise, and personalize all that is given here. Jazz music is highly creative, very personal, and ever-changing. Therefore this book is an attempt to hit a moving target, and for all the experience that has gone into the notions presented here, it is nevertheless the expression of one person's opinion.

Because jazz programs are proliferating at a considerable pace, many conversations and appeals are taking place between institutional administrators and hopeful leaders of jazz programs. It is hoped that the following passages will not only help the would-be jazz educator, but also prove useful in convincing others of the need for jazz programs.

What Is Jazz?

Definitions of jazz exist copiously in dictionaries and in virtually all books that have been written on the history of jazz. It is not the intent here to add still another encyclopedic/historical definition of the music, but to list elemental aspects which describe the music in its present state. That it was born in America nearly a century ago and has enjoyed genius level practitioners of the likes of Louis Armstrong, Duke Ellington, Miles Davis, Charlie Parker, and John Coltrane, are foregone conclusions that are understood by most musicians of any musical style. Likewise it is unnecessary to elucidate here on the historical development of jazz by stylistic periods.

(1) jazz is a musical art form, recognized as such around the world;
(2) the key element of jazz is the craft of improvisation;
(3) improvisation is a musical *skill*, requiring considerable time to develop. The theory and musical tools of improvisation may be mentally understood in a relatively short space of time, but the honing of the performance skills requires years. Successful levels of performance might be reached within a few years, but mastery is elusive and the improviser who continues to practice continues to improve for a lifetime;
(4) jazz is a very creative, personal sort of music. It is a musical democracy in which diverse approaches abound and are generally accepted. Though there are traditions and common-sense elements, the individual has the relative freedom to express himself/herself at will with respect to the utilization of the tradition;
(5) jazz is highly communicative and extremely spontaneous in that

communication. The highest level of group jazz performance requires that the individual members listen carefully to one another to the point of being able to spontaneously produce music that has collective merit and creates a unified whole. Even the audience can affect the musical outcome through their response, their musical tastes, and by their sheer numbers or lack of same;

(6) as a musical style, jazz is very elusive, often confounding the critics, entrepreneurs, and audiences when they try to label and categorize the music as jazz or non-jazz. Some feel that the music is only jazz if it contains improvisation. Many feel that rhythmic swing and/or jazz phrasing are the determining factors. Others feel that the only jazz is a particular style within jazz, such as dixieland. Still others are liable to call *any* music jazz that is not classical music; and

(7) elements of the jazz style have permeated nearly all known musical styles and musical functions. Similarly, the 'open door policy' of jazz has caused the music to absorb and reflect elements of virtually all non-jazz styles, yet retain a sort of diverse identity.

Rationale for the Adoption of Jazz Programs in the University

This raises three important questions:

(1) Can jazz be taught?
(2) Why should it be taught?
(3) Why should jazz programs be housed in the university setting?

Addressing the first question, the answer is "yes". Despite the many myths and spoken clichés about jazz, like "You either got it or you ain't", "If you have to ask, don't mess with it", "Jazz can't be taught any more than composition can be taught", or "Teaching jazz creates a sterile product", the fact is that within this author's lifetime a multitude of effective methods and teaching tools have been created and developed for the teaching of jazz. Great numbers of successful jazz artists have benefited from those methods and tools already. Only the uninformed will continue to believe that jazz cannot be taught.

As to *why* it should be taught, jazz is listened to, documented, and admired internationally (i.e. Japan, Europe, Australia, and New Zealand, to mention just a few), and if the reader is American, jazz is generally referred to as "America's only original art form". Consider also that because jazz, stylistically, encompasses so many musical styles and has had far-reaching influences on those styles, it has become a sort of stylistic center of music (see point 7 of "What Is Jazz?"). Therefore jazz education provides a very practical type of training for budding professional musicians. Finally, the teaching techniques of jazz, in their presently developed state, offer a unique brand of training found nowhere else in non-jazz music programs, and those new techniques engender a well-rounded sort of musicianship.

Question 3 ("Why should jazz programs be housed in the university setting?") is a more complex question. We could simply point out that it has been tried and proven to be successful. But it would be unfair to ignore the alternatives altogether. One of those alternatives, which could be described as 'the school of hard knocks' or 'street learning' suggests that the best way to learn to play jazz is by listening, observation, experience, trial and error, imitation, etc. These are *all* valid notions and should be incorporated into the jazz learning experience, certainly. After all, how did all the great players of pre-jazz education years learn their craft? Can we improve on that? First of all, be reminded that modern jazz education does *not* ignore the methods of 'street learning'. Secondly, the genius of an Armstrong, a Parker, or a Coltrane, for example, was such that nothing could have deterred them from their musical goals, including the lack of a formal or organized jazz education. The same could be said of Wes Montgomery and Ira Sullivan. They were all blessed with a special gift. As Bobby

McFerrin said when accepting his Grammy award in 1987 (quoting James 1:17), "Every good and perfect gift is from above, coming down from the Father of the heavenly lights". But God-given gifts must be practiced and developed*. With genius there is the obsessive quality of striving to excel, and the willingness to persevere against all odds. But that is not to say that they would have ignored institutionalized jazz education, had it been available, or that their creative output would have been impaired if they had been exposed to excellent university study. We'll never know what impact a quality jazz education *might* have had on their playing, if any. At the very least, however, their development may have been slightly accelerated, or perhaps a few more musical options may have become available to them in their quest for consummate expression, through interaction with other gifted students and the opportunity to use students, facilities, and audiences to test their output.

Remember, too, that a truly good system of jazz education relies heavily on the retrospective observation of all that we can glean from those great artists, through listening, transcription, analysis, and imitation. For example, careful observation of Coltrane's improvisations on "Giant Steps" taught us that he utilized digital patterns to cope with that swiftly-moving and perpetually modulating chord progression. Hence, many teachers of improvisation will assign such patterns to their students and apply them to similar progressions, as part of their development.

Is jazz to be performed only by geniuses? Surely not, as much great music has been produced by players who were *initially* less-endowed, and *they* could benefit from the opportunity to work and learn in a good jazz program. Often, elements of genius are awakened as a result of study and practice. Some believe that gifts can be received by faith,

* McFerrin also said in a masterclass lecture at the University of Tennessee that he started preparation of improvisation with Patterns for Jazz (Coker, Casale, Campbell and Greene, Columbia Pictures Publications).

or by visualization (we can picture virtuosity or success, or absorb it by association).

Let's examine another alternative to the university jazz program: private instruction. Such instruction has advantages, to be sure. For one thing, it is a one-on-one situation, which promotes individual attention. For another, you can select the teacher of your preference, whereas in the university program that selection may be made by someone else. The disadvantages would include cost, availability (not all master players can or want to teach), lack of consistency (due to transient players/teachers, plus the fact that private students tend to be irregular without the pressure of their parent's financial commitment or a course grade), the lack of group study (which has definite advantages at times), and the likelihood that private study will have a narrower scope, perhaps limited to one subject. Nevertheless private study, under the right circumstances, is a viable alternative to university programs. There are pluses and minuses for university jazz programs, too. They offer a broader education and a degree (perhaps), but the student will also be forced to take non-music courses that dilute the area of concentration, and universities are frought with inflexible policies. Remember, though, that university jazz programs do not ignore private study, any more than the useful techniques of 'street learning', and non-jazz and even non-music courses *can* be *supportive* of jazz study, if chosen carefully.

Finally, the university setting offers space, facilities, equipment, a thorough-going educational plan, time for practice, and the opportunity to interact with many of the peer group. With respect to the latter, the original Pat Metheny Quartet, for example, included Mark Egan and Danny Gottlieb, schoolmates of Metheny in the University of Miami jazz program. Lyle Mays was the only member of the quartet who wasn't an ex-Miami student.

Now we should examine the reasons why a university should be interested in housing a jazz program. On the purely practical side:

(1) jazz programs are popular, drawing large numbers of good new students. To this author's knowledge, no jazz program has ever needed to be suspended for lack of enrollees;

(2) courses like jazz history are likely to draw 50-250 students each time the courses are offered, yet they can be taught by one teacher, yielding an enviable 50:1-250:1 student-to-teacher ratio; and

(3) jazz programs bring good publicity to the university. They help create a needed image of progress, artistic vitality, and a positive response to a changing world, leading to more community interest and support. Jazz programs also lead to more articles in student and city newspapers. Finally, strong jazz ensembles can attend festivals, achieve honors of distinction, and might be invited to perform abroad for the State Department.

The foregoing list emphasizes the revenue-oriented benefits. But there are other important considerations. Jazz programs tend to draw students who have well-defined goals and who are amenable to and interested in *all* musical styles. Jazz courses also attract non-jazz and non-music students, especially in courses like jazz history, jazz piano classes, and jazz ensembles. All this creates a more integrated, unified student body. Furthermore the jazz courses taken by non-jazz music majors enhance their preparedness for the modern world of music, giving them greater flexibility and understanding. The non-jazz piano major taking jazz piano courses, for example, is better prepared for both professional performance and with a greater musical understanding for teaching. The music education major who enrolls in jazz pedagogy, jazz directing, jazz ensembles, improvisation, or jazz arranging is better prepared to handle a high school jazz ensemble, which may be a part of his/her duties as a bandmaster.

Jazz programs also tend to inspire and revitalize members of the non-jazz music faculty of the university, presenting them with new challenges in working with the generally inquisitive nature of the jazz majors who come into their theory, musicology, and applied courses.

Also, some of the non-jazz faculty may become inspired by contributing to the jazz program itself, if they've had an abiding interest in the style even before the program was begun. Such activity may also provide another option for filling out the teaching loads of non-jazz teachers who, temporarily perhaps, have a diminished load (especially applied teachers, whose teaching loads are largely determined by the influx and graduation rate of students who major in specific instruments).

Perhaps the most important consideration of all lies in the area of job training and the job market. If a university really cares about the future of its graduates, then it cannot afford to ignore this question. Those in the university music school environment have traditionally been sheltered from the real world, burying themselves in old books, old music, old methods, old values, etc. Sometimes this is because there is the love of the past more than the present; sometimes, in order to protect personal turf; sometimes, because of resistance against learning the newer ways; and sometimes out of sheer ignorance of current trends. And so, many music schools continue, as my old friend and colleague Alfred Reed once put it, "to manufacture the world's greatest buggy whips in a world that is no longer buying many buggy whips." In 1970 Reed presented figures showing that 95% of the monies spent by this nation's music schools is spent on a musical style that hires only 6% of its graduates. Now no one is saying that everything old is worthless, nor that everything new is greater than everything old. None of us wants to abandon the great cultural/sociological traditions of the past, like symphonies, operas, chamber music, piano concerti, etc., but we don't want to mislead our students or overproduce, either. On one hand we see the need to subsidize our orchestras; abandon hopes of earning a living as a touring concert artist; compete with 500 others for one position in a professional orchestra (whose members need to supplement their salaries by 'moonlighting'); or realize that gaining a position with an opera company is next to impossible. Even finding a career as a high school bandmaster isn't as easy as it used to be, thanks to our over-production of music education graduates, coupled with alarming budgetary cutbacks in funding of the arts in most school districts.

On the other hand we have facts like those delivered in David Baskerville's momentous keynote address to the full assembly of the 1968 convention of the National Association of Schools of Music, in which he scathingly reported that there is a 4-8 billion dollar per year music industry going on in which we've played no part. He also went on to cite true cases in which a pianist with a Ph.D. in piano performance was unable to function in his first record date because he couldn't read chord symbols, and a young woman with a masters degree in music education who had to confess to her ghetto school music class that she'd never heard of James Brown! They both lost their jobs.

Most universities have been trying to operate with a hiring freeze imposed upon them for the past 15-20 years. Yet a great number of them have wisely added jazz degree programs (see Preface) during that time, usually by changing job descriptions of departing or retiring faculty members. In other words, there is a market for jazz instructors. One has only to watch for announcements of teaching positions each winter and spring to know that this is true. There are also announcements of position vacancies for non-jazz instructors, like theory, musicology, and applied music, but as in the case of announcements for positions in symphony orchestras, you can expect that there will be many qualified applicants, as we have over-produced in those areas, too. Jazz programs are proliferating at a rapid pace, it is a relatively new area of study, and very few institutions have been training students to *teach* jazz. Therefore, there is a unique demand for teachers of jazz, especially teachers who can organize and lead new jazz programs.

Furthermore, there is a shortage of qualified graduate assistants for jazz programs, and graduate assistantships are an effective means of proving one's worth, which *could* lead to an offer of employment in a jazz program.

This author has often wondered how universities can display signs on buildings such as ***Music Building***, ***School of Music***, or ***Department of Music***, when in most cases, only *one* style of music is actually offered. Under such circumstances, would it not be more honest and accurate to display signs which read ***School of European Music***, ***Department of Traditional Music***, or ***Classical Music Building***? A surprising number of young musicans are confused and disappointed to learn that a university department calls itself a 'music department', though it is incapable of, even hostile toward, teaching them to sing in a popular style, play guitar in a country style, or play saxophone in a jazz style, for example. They're often disappointed, too, to learn that a university will retain a violin teacher who has only several students, yet offer no instruction in guitar, saxophone, banjo, mandolin, or electric bass (*all* very popular instruments in the outside world): Isn't it time for music departments to learn to distinguish musical *quality* judgements from musical *style* judgements? Styles need not be judged as good or poor, or as valid or invalid. Within *any* musical style (including European classical music) we find varying levels of quality, from good to poor.

They also wonder why the department expects pianists to practice on the school's old, battered upright pianos, when the student is likely to own a Yamaha DX-7 synthesizer, a Fender Rhodes keyboard, or a PF-88. And many students, even non-music students, have better stereo and taping facilities in their dormitory rooms than the university provides for the classrooms, studios, and libraries in which music is so diligently studied. Music is *sound*. If the university community wishes to be regarded as musical experts, then they must concern themselves with the quality of the tools of *teaching* music. The quality of a playback system, for example, should be regarded as being of equal importance as the quality of the musical instruments the teachers select for themselves and their students.

To conclude this segment of the chapter, we should briefly discuss the relative *cost* of operating jazz programs, which is a natural concern of the university. The fact is that, compared to the cost of operating most other music programs, the jazz program is extremely inexpensive. From the standpoint of staffing, one good, well-rounded jazz instructor can handle all the jazz courses needed by jazz majors, until the number of majors exceeds 20 or 30, and graduate assistants can enable that number to reach approximately 40-50 majors before needing additional faculty. Furthermore the budget for music, books, records, and equipment for a jazz program can be surprisingly small. It goes without saying that a program that is properly staffed and funded will be a better program. The point is, a jazz program is relatively inexpensive to put in place and operate on a continuing basis.

Who Should Teach Jazz?

Every human being, from the time he/she comes into this world, is continually bombarded with the need to make decisions and choices. Some choices are relatively trivial, like: "What shall I wear today?" "What brand of toothpaste should I buy?" "Do I want a Coke or a Pepsi (or neither!)" Other decisions are of considerably more importance, like: "What should I eat?" "Should I take drugs?" "What should be my spiritual path?" "If a pregnancy results from this association, am I ready to assume the responsibility?" Even being happy or unhappy, productive or unproductive, brilliant or dull, and being healthy or unhealthy are, in large part at least, a matter of choice. Amidst such a plethora of choices, one of the most important, though not the most important, is the choice of life's work... a suitable occupation. The average person sleeps eight hours at night and will spend about three more hours with preparing for meals (buying food, cooking, washing dishes, or driving to restaurants) and consuming them. Perhaps another two hours is spent with bathing, grooming, and dressing, and yet another hour or more spent communicating with others /family, telephone, etc.). So of the remaining ten or so hours, most people are plying their chosen occupation for an average of eight hours per day (plus commuting time). We don't exactly choose to sleep, eat, groom, and communicate, though we can adjust the time spent on them, so our occupation consumes about 80% of the time with which we do have a choice with regard to the nature of the activity. Therefore, such a decision is one of the most crucial faced by most human beings. A wrong decision can be disastrous, resulting, perhaps, in boredom, frustration, depression, and the likelihood of poor rendering of service to others. The ironic fact is that most people are expected to make such a choice very early, responding to pressures from parents, peer groups, economics, and the educational institutions they attend. All too often, as stated in the preface, young people enter the field of teaching for the wrong reasons. Many students major in music education because they've decided that their chances of survival in the professional world of music performance are too slim. They might come to such a conclusion because they sense a lack of innate ability, or they've discovered that they don't want to put in the long hours of practice, or perhaps they've lost faith in their country's desire to support, upgrade, and participate in its musical culture. But all of these reasons are negative in nature; that is, anyone using such reasons for their decision to enter music education does so because they wish to avoid something, namely the competitive field of performance, not because they believe deeply in the ideals of music education, feel especially qualified to be a good teacher, and sincerely want to be of service to young people in their discovery of the joys of music. We frequently hear the phrase, "If I don't succeed as a performer, I can always fall back on teaching." Such a statement shows a lack of self-confidence and commitment toward becoming a performer, indicates that they view teaching as a lesser choice of vocation, and implies that anyone can teach, regardless of their qualifications and interests. A similar statement, also very commonly used, is "Those who can, do; those who cannot, teach."

Even the training received by music education students is subject to question. Such students are frequently given a curriculum that de-emphasizes applied lessons, theory, composition, arranging, and piano (for non-pianists), all of which could make for more knowledgeable, creative teachers. Yet such a curriculum is very likely to include courses which train students to plot marching formations for half-time shows at football games. Unfortunately, the latter will become the gravest responsibility of the high school bandmaster trainees. This points up a serious deficiency in the way we, as a country, have failed to introduce and train the very young in music. Instead of teaching music to young students, we *use* them to put on shows for athletic events. It is this author's contention that such exploitation of their time and talent causes many young musicians to turn away from music, culturally and occupationally. This is not to say that marching bands are valueless; they entertain audiences and provide a reasonable amount of fun for the participants. But such an activity should not have become the sum total of a young person's exposure to music.

Teaching should be done by people who recognize that teaching is a *skill*, and are willing to devote the time and effort to *continually* hone that skill, in behalf of their students. *Music* teaching should be done by people who, in addition to recognizing that teaching is a skill, love music, are capable performers, and are devoted to being a perpetual student of music. *Jazz* music teaching should be done by people who, in addition to all of the foregoing, are uncommonly versatile (they may need to teach many different subjects within the idiom) and are devoted to continually learning the many new trends of a young, ever-changing, highly creative musical style. It is very unlikely that a jazz educator, even a very good one, will realize much fame or fortune. Service is the name of the game. The rewards are watching creative, young people blossom and develop, and in the personal reward of knowing that the teacher is continually learning and developing, too.

This author once asked all members of a jazz pedagogy class to submit a list of what they considered to be the most important qualities of a jazz educator. The resulting composite list revealed some interesting revelations. They listed more *personal* qualities than musical qualities, and they were more in accord with the personal qualities than the musical ones, too. For example, 100% of the students said the good jazz educator should have a positive attitude, have an energetic, encouraging, motivating, and inspiring effect on the students, and have a sense of humor. Yet only 60% listed that the jazz educator should have a thorough knowledge of the subject matter, methods, and materials! The point is not that they didn't all list knowledge as the most important factor, but that they were more concerned about the personal qualities, especially the ones mentioned here. The other personal qualities listed, though not in 100% agreement, were: patience; open-mindedness; a modest attitude toward self; the desire to continue learning; communicative skills; literacy; responsibility; organizational skills; aggression; industry; love of the work; idealism toward work; accessibility; friendliness; respectfulness (of student opinions); appreciation for and acknowledgement of, the efforts of other teachers in the program; and poise (listed in the order of decreasing percentages). The musical qualities listed were knowledge of all musical styles, professional playing experience, exceptionally good musical ears, command of an instrument, ability to demonstrate examples for classes, and professional arranging/composing experience.

In closing this chapter, it is appropriate to distinguish between jazz performers, jazz teachers, and jazz program leadership. A jazz performer is not necessarily a good teacher... some are not. But such performers, especially if they are gifted, can still function as performance models and are needed in that respect. Their position in the program might be viewed as artists-in-residence, focusing more on performances, demonstrations, and perhaps coaching some student ensembles. The jazz teacher can be more involved with teaching specific classes and ensembles. The leader of a jazz program will, hopefully, have performing ability, be a capable teacher of most or all of the jazz courses, plus have the ability and willingness to conceptualize the jazz program, organize the jazz faculty and lead their activities, recruit and advise students, promote the program, and act as liason between the jazz program and the various levels of administration. Since many jazz programs, especially new ones, are likely to be one-man programs for at least awhile, the following list may aid the reader in learning the duties of the jazz program leader:

CURRICULUM WORK
Design curriculum.
Revise curriculum, when necessary.
Add new courses.
(all of the above require completing of university forms, writing catalog descriptions, attending university committee meetings, deciding who will teach courses, selecting and ordering texts, scheduling of courses into particular school terms and clock times and rooms, etc.).

CLASS/REHEARSAL PREPARATION
Devise syllabi.
Create audio-visual materials (teaching tapes, dubbing of tapes, hand-outs, writing lead lines/changes, material for library reserve shelves, arranging/composing material for ensembles, listening and/or transcribing tapes and records of new music, etc.).
Review new books (as possible texts) and published arrangements (for ensembles).

CLERICAL WORK
Xeroxing.
Filing (hand-outs, lead lines, arrangements, official forms, tapes, records, etc.).
Filling out university forms.
Fielding phone calls.
Correspondence (inquiries, notes to faculty, letters of recommendation, etc.).

COUNSELING
Student advising and counseling.
Interviews with prospective students and others.
Create policy guideline papers for students and jazz faculty.

MEETINGS
Jazz majors.
Jazz faculty.
Department faculty.
Departmental and university committees.

CALENDAR WORK
Plan and schedule concerts, recitals, meetings, clinics, guest artists, and off-campus activities.
Reserve concert/recital hall, classrooms for special events..

EVALUATIONS
Grades.
Juries.
Proficiencies.
Auditions (new students, ensembles)
Recital hearings.
Recital adjudication.

PUBLISHING
Write articles for professional journals.
Create brochures and flyers for program.
Be interviewed for articles.
Public relations activities.

OFF-CAMPUS ACTIVITIES
Concerts.
Clinics/lectures.
Adjudication at festivals.
Attend conventions (perhaps to operate a booth, as well).
Recruiting.

2

The Jazz Curriculum

The most frequently asked question by prospective jazz majors and/or their parents, is "What is the practical value of a degree in jazz?" This question is usually followed by another question; "Will it lead to gainful employment?" The concern is understandable, but the questions are not very logical. No degree plan guarantees a future in the field. A degree is not a license that assures the holder of a job. It is more like a fishing license or a parking sticker for a parking lot that does not assign parking spaces, in that they license you to fish or hunt for a space, but there are no guarantees that you will catch fish or that you will find a place to put your car. Nonetheless you pay for the license as a first step in your quest and to avoid the penalties for not having one. If you are a skilled fisherman, or if you show up early at the parking lot, your chances for success are greatly increased. All university degrees are like this. A law degree may seem very practical, but the student must still study diligently and pass a bar exam before hanging out a shingle. A medical degree is viewed as practical, but again the student must meet the rigors of the study, attend school for a longer period of time than most degrees, and serve as an intern before he/she can begin a practice and begin charging patients for the cost of attaining the degree and the cost of opening a practice. In music, jazz is perhaps the most practical field of all, if the training and the study meet reasonable standards. This owes largely to the fact that jazz study is more broad in stylistic scope and in functional scope (producing graduates who can play more than one instrument, compose and arrange, improvise, teach, conduct, etc.) and the fact that the field itself is more popular, larger, broader in stylistic scope, and is not glutted with qualified but unemployed degree holders to the extent that we find in classical music performance, opera, and school band conducting (discussed in Chapter 1). In other words, the value of any degree plan derives from the training and study encountered while seeking the degree, not from the piece of paper that is delivered upon completion of the plan. It is pure myth, not fact, that a great musician who is prepared for today's world of music is subject to being overlooked, unemployed, or starving to death. Such a musician can defeat themselves through their behavior, to be sure, but success will not be denied them for musical reasons. There are five important conditions which, if met, can reasonably assure success to persons preparing for the field of music:

(1) enter an area of music that is not glutted;
(2) choose a school that offers an excellent curriculum (courses and sequence of courses);
(3) choose a school that has an excellent teaching staff for the curriculum;
(4) learn to be versatile; and
(5) work hard enough to assimilate the attributes of the curriculum and the teaching staff, and to develop your God-given talents to their fullest extent.

Problems To Be Faced

Once a university opts to add jazz to its list of possible majors, it would be logical to presume that the rest of the planning and initiating of the curriculum would simply be a matter of having a qualified jazz educator list the courses needed and place them in a sensible sequence. Logical, yes, but unfortunately untrue. Like most agencies and institutions, the university is an enormous bureaucracy, with a plethora of administrators, committees, clerical workers, policies, records, budgets, forms, reports, etc., with new ones added on a regular basis. Ideally, education is the simple process of a teacher meeting with his/her students. If they could meet out-of-doors or at the teacher's home, the process would remain simple. Instead, a third party is brought into the process, a sort of landlord who provides the meeting place for the teacher and the students. The rest is simple. The landlord runs amuck, invents thousands of new rules and regulations, hires many new people to help him enforce the policies he's invented, raises the rent (tuition), gets caught up in the glory of his new-found leadership (which can be passed on from generation to generation), which causes his share of the student's money to be increased, and eventually he has to try to explain to the teacher and his students why it is that there isn't enough money for the needs of education.

Perhaps the foregoing is simplistic and exaggerated, and an administrator would object strenuously, pointing out that the university needs leadership, records must be kept, legal services must be provided, dormitories and dining halls must be operated, a campus police force must be used to maintain order, counseling services must be provided for the student, etc. But the tail is wagging the dog. Webster defines education as "the process of training and developing the knowledge, skill, mind, character, etc., especially by formal schooling, teaching, training." Webster adds three more definitions of the word, but nowhere is there mention of administrative function or duties. Unquestionably we need administrators in the university, but we must retain the basic notion of the definition of education. Put another way, if the students should decide not to attend school tomorrow and/or the teachers decide not to meet their students, education ceases to exist, and the landlord loses his function, position, wealth, and power immediately. None of this is likely to happen, but the thought should be sufficient to sustain our perspective on the definition of education and the relationship of the student, teacher, and administrator to that definition.

Our first problem, then, in setting up a jazz curriculum, is contending with a very slow-moving bureaucracy. The curriculum proposal must be carefully entered on a myriad of university forms and presented to many committees for approval, a process which can easily consume a year's time, and the program may not appear in the printed university catalog until two years after the process was begun.

The second problem has to do with pre-existing conditions that would affect any new curriculum. The prevailing university philosophy recognizes that the average student needs certain basic knowledge and skills, apart from his/her major area, which will better prepare them for their future. Given a choice, the student might attempt to avoid certain subjects, for one reason or another, only to discover later in life that he/she should have been more willing to meet the challenge of studying a practical, if difficult, subject. So, to protect the student and to maintain the credibility of the institution's methods and responsibilities, the university will require that all students, regardless of their major area, will take certain courses or course areas which the university feels would prove useful to all of its graduates. These might include subjects like English, history, a foreign language, and mathematics, and courses which must be selected by the student from certain areas of study, such as humanities, social science, natural science, etc. There is an accompanying danger that, because the courses are required of all students and therefore have perpetually large enrollments, the quality of instruction may suffer and/or students may become discouraged about university study from being force-fed with courses that don't interest them, or are ineffectual.

Then, too, the music department will also feel that certain music courses should be taken by all music majors, regardless of their major area within music. Such required courses might include music theory, music history, participation in certain ensembles, musical analysis, orchestration, and conducting. The problem is not that the university or the music department require certain courses. For example, the alarming rise of illiteracy in this country points to a definite need to require courses in English (and that such courses are taught with greater effectiveness!). And all musicians need to study music theory and music history. The problem is that when the university and the music department have finished their long lists of required courses, there is but little space remaining on the student's study load for investigating the major area itself! For the jazz educator, this sort of curriculum crowding leads to the necessity of devising jazz courses that have to be offered for one or two credit hours, instead of three or four. For the students in the jazz program, the resulting effect is that they must enroll for perhaps ten courses per term in order to amass a total of only sixteen credit hours, which means that their study of all courses is diluted by the sheer effort of meeting the classes and class assignments of ten courses per term!

The Jazz Curriculum

Since universities and music departments within universities will vary, with respect to required non-jazz courses, the individual jazz educator will need to carefully assess the possible quantity of jazz course offerings, what topics can be included, how many terms may be devoted to those topics, and what number of credit hours may be assigned to each course. With this in mind, the following discussion will not specify the numbers of credit hours.Furthermore the list of courses needed will represent the minimum number. A supplementary list of other possible courses will be provided after the initial list for those jazz educators who are fortunate enough to be able to add to the basic list.

The following is a basic list of jazz courses proven effective at several leading universities. The courses are listed in the approximate order of presentation to the student. An asterisk has been placed next to courses which should be continued for two or more school terms. If the course title is not self-explanatory, a very brief description of the course activities appears in parenthesis.

History of Jazz
Jazz Theory (chord/scale nomenclature, chord progression tendencies, and ear-training)
Analysis of Jazz Styles (transcribing and analyzing improvised solos)
Jazz Piano (for pianists **and non-pianists)*
** Jazz Improvisation*
Jazz Composition (melody and progression writing, study of models)
**Jazz Arranging (small and large ensembles)*
Junior Recital (jazz)
** Advanced Improvisation*
Jazz Pedagogy
Senior Recital (jazz)

Note: Jazz ensembles, large and small, should be taken in every term, throughout the curriculum.

A term-by-term plan might look like the following:

FIRST YEAR

Fall -	*Jazz History*
	Jazz Piano I
Spring -	*Jazz Theory*
	Jazz Piano II

SECOND YEAR

Fall - *Jazz Improvisation I*
Analysis of Jazz Styles
Spring - *Jazz Improvisation II*

THIRD YEAR

Fall - *Jazz Composition*
Spring - *Jazz Arranging I*
Junior Recital (jazz)

FOURTH YEAR

Fall - *Advanced Improvisation I*
Jazz Arranging II
Spring - *Advanced Improvisation II*
Jazz Pedagogy
Senior Recital (jazz)

Although there is room for variation in the order or sequencing of the jazz courses, the above order follows a natural unfolding of subject matter for the student. The History of Jazz is needed early in the curriculum, since even the well-attuned freshman jazz major is likely to have listened to only a handful of jazz performers, and most of those will be current, present-day players. For them the history course will expose them to the rich heritage left to us by great performers of a style that is nearly a century old, and will enable them to see the link between the techniques and styles of the past and those of the present. Most of all, they will be led to discoveries of players that will further inspire them, players they might never have heard were it not for the jazz history course. For the less-attuned student, who may be a marginal music student or a crossover from another style (rock, concert band, country, etc.), the course will either help them in their adjustment or simply serve to apprise them of a musical style that may not be their calling. At least they will have been exposed to the music early enough to change majors with little loss of time. Another reason for placing the jazz history course early in the curriculum stems from the need to use what they learn about the jazz style during such a course to help them interpret the music they play in large and small jazz ensembles. Some jazz educators feel that jazz history should be expanded into two or more courses for jazz majors, perhaps following the basic course with a more penetrating one, or to concentrate on more modern styles. Some feel that, since the basic course might be taken by a wide variety of students (non-jazz music students and non-music students), perhaps a different, more penetrating course in jazz history should be offered to jazz majors instead of the basic course. In any event, at least the first jazz history course should be taken very early in the curriculum.

Jazz Theory should also be scheduled early in the curriculum, as it introduces the student to the complex harmonic language of jazz, a topic which will engage his/her musical thoughts throughout courses like improvisation and arranging. Therefore the basics of the language need to be presented early in study. The course also serves two other important functions. It weeds out the less-serious students and prepares the remainder for improvisation courses of the second year, as improvisation courses need to be protected from needlessly high enrollments and time lost while explaining the simpler aspects of the harmonic language. Again, the jazz theory course will also help the improvising efforts of students in the jazz ensembles.

Throughout the jazz curriculum, no course is as desperately needed as the Jazz Piano courses, and if it is taught effectively, no course has more practical value nor can any other course project more usable skills in such a short time*. Players of all instruments need to be able to use the keyboard as a tool for learning courses like Jazz Theory, Jazz Improvisation, Jazz Composition, Jazz Arranging, etc. Some will find it to be a teaching tool as well, some will find that they can use piano as a secondary instrument in professional performances, and a few will even switch to piano as their concentration instrument as a result of taking the jazz piano course. Therefore the Jazz Piano sequence should also be begun early in the curriculum. It has been this author's experience that even the jazz majors who are pianists are not likely, as freshmen, to know the techniques taught in the jazz piano courses.

By the second year of study in the curriculum presented here, the student has listened to a lot of jazz (jazz history), learned the basic theory and nomenclature (jazz theory), and acquired a useful tool for studying and ingraining the harmonic language of jazz (jazz piano). The second year, then, is the logical time to begin the study of improvisation. If the courses in improvisation had been offered in the first year, too much class time would have been lost with explanations of harmonic principles, and the students would not yet have formed a sufficient stylistic conception for creating a solo in the style (with respect to the latter, the student is helped toward a jazz conception in the first year via jazz history, participation in jazz ensembles, and listening to others in their peer group who are a little more experienced). If improvisation were not offered until the third year, it might not occur in time to help them in their improvisational work in jazz ensembles, nor would it allow sufficient time to hone their improvisational skills (which takes more time than merely comprehending the subject matter) before the advanced improvisation courses, recitals, and graduation. Some jazz educators feel that some sort of improvisation course should be scheduled in the first year, even if it might need to be a very basic course (modal tunes, playing by ear, playing jazz

* (p. 38) JAZZ KEYBOARD (Coker) is a time-tested method which is easily learned and can be taught by non-pianists, and which has produced consistent success with students who are non-pianists as well as trained pianists.

melodies, etc.), in the interest of exposing the student to the skill a little earlier. It is doubtful that anyone would question the merit of a freshman year course in basic improvisation. It is more likely that the problem may be one stemming from the lack of available credit hours and clock hours. If it is not a problem, then a first year improvisation course would improve the curriculum. But such a course should not replace any part of the second year's courses in improvisation, where it will be found that no time can be spared without sacrificing some of the objectives.

Throughout the planning of the jazz curriculum the person(s) responsible for that curriculum will be faced with important decisions of the nature just described, owing to the previously discussed problem of finding enough credit hours for the major area of study. Many good ideas for additional jazz courses will come to mind for which credit hours, clock hours, space, and teaching time cannot be found. We can only try.

Little needs to be said at this time about the importance of the improvisation courses contained in the second year, as most jazz educators would agree that improvisation is the most essential element of jazz performance, as well as the most challenging aspect of the player's development. It is a skill, and therefore must be begun early and practiced diligently for a lifetime. Hence the objective of the second year's courses in improvisation should not be to bring the needed skills to full fruition by the end of the second year (a most unreasonable goal), but to introduce the student to the myriad of traditions and techniques of the craft, begin their application, and render a modus operandi for perpetual study and practice.

The other course in the second year is Analysis of Jazz Styles. Now it was mentioned earlier that no course has more practical value nor project more usable skills in such a short time as jazz piano courses. But a very close contender for that description is Analysis of Jazz Styles. Though a brief course (1 term), it teaches the language of jazz even more swiftly than improvisation (because it is analysis, rather than a gradual introduction of skills), teaches the student to assess and appreciate the values of solos by major improvisers, launches their efforts in transcribing solos, and quickly trains their ears to perceive and understand the sounds around them (even without the benefit of a formal, written transcription, much of the time!). The fact that the course is concomitantly offered with improvisation, the focus of the latter is enhanced considerably.

The third year contains two of the three music writing courses, Jazz Composition and Jazz Arranging I. These were withheld from the first two years because of the demands upon the student's theoretical knowledge, his/her need for some stylistic maturity, the need of having developed enough scholarly skills to complete time-consuming projects, and the needed ability and penmanship to commit one's musical thoughts to paper. The non-jazz music courses required by the music department (such as theory, ear-training, analysis, orchestration, etc.) are probably more supportive of the student's study of jazz composition and arranging than of any of the other jazz courses, and most or all of those non-jazz courses would have been completed by the third year, or at least concurrently with the jazz writing courses. The primary reason for not placing the jazz writing courses in the fourth year, where the student would be even better prepared, is the need to hear and have performed the music they compose and/or arrange, which is no easy task after graduation, but quite available before graduation, thanks to a number of capable, friendly, rehearsing jazz ensembles of various sizes and instrumentation within the university program. Another reason is to allow some of the more gifted writers to contribute to the repertoire of those ensembles, which would be somewhat limited if the jazz writing courses were not offered until the fourth year.

In this educator's opinion, the chief function of the Jazz Composition course is to teach the basics of writing, rather than to attempt massive, extended scores. Such basic study could include:

(1) study and appreciation of many great tunes, pin-pointing the most appealing aspects of each;
(2) learning to re-write the rhythms of standard tune melodies;
(3) learning re-harmonization and chord substitution techniques;
(4) study of melodic form;
(5) composing of reasonably effective chord progressions;
(6) composing of tunes of various types, such as blues, modal, bebop, contemporary, fusion, etc., aimed at enlarging the student's creative scope.

The third year course in arranging should probably focus on composing/arranging for the small ensemble, learning basic harmonization techniques for 2-5 parts, writing for the rhythm section, experimenting with formal design, learning instrumental ranges and idiosyncracies, and learning to prepare a score.

Finally, the third year should contain a junior recital in jazz, or perhaps a half-recital or a joint recital with another junior student in the jazz program. Such a performance might have several objectives. One would be to check each student's progress before entering the final year of study. In this respect, some schools require each student to pass several levels of proficiencies in topics such as sight-reading, improvisation, scales, and perhaps voicings and progression-reading for pianists and guitarists, bass line construction for bassists, and various beat-styles for drummers, all to be completed before scheduling a recital. A recital hearing 2-3 weeks before a scheduled recital is also sound practice, enabling the faculty to determine the readiness of the student and his/her assisting personnel to deliver a creditable recital. Another reason for junior recital is to afford an opportunity for the student to develop organizational and musical leadership, as he/she is responsible for the selection of the materials, the arrangement of that material, establishing a logical program order, selecting and preparing assisting personnel, scheduling and leading rehearsals and the recital itself, producing a printed program, handling advertising and promotion for the recital, and being responsible for all physical and electronic equipment for the performance hall (staging, lighting, attire, sound equipment, recording equipment, etc.). Needless to say, the student who learns to cope with all these details will be better prepared for the professional world of music, especially for those times when he/she is the designated leader of the group's engagement. A final reason for the junior recital would be to promote the chances for an even better senior recital in the fourth year, the student having learned many lessons and perhaps overcome some of the uneasiness of public performance by having given the junior recital.

The courses of the fourth year (Advanced Improvisation, Jazz Arranging II, Jazz Pedagogy, and Senior Recital) are all courses which would be inappropriate during the first three years. The second year course in improvisation, because skills are involved, will most assuredly leave many 'loose ends', many techniques and skills unmastered. This is the logic behind leaving the third year devoid of improvisation courses, so that the student has the opportunity to engage in a sort of 'mop-up campaign' on his/her own time, reviewing what was presented and partially applied and ingrained in the second year, and working toward greater assimilation and relative mastery of those 'loose ends'. In this way the student will be better prepared to take Advanced Improvisation, which can focus on problems that would have been unreasonable in the second year's course, such as learning to play melodies and improvise tunes in 12 keys, playing very bright tempos, improvising at sight on 'new' tunes, layering devices, chord substitutions, and new progressions over the given progressions, the study of symmetrical intervals in improvisation, a deeper penetration into contemporary vehicles, learning to play over drones, and an emphasis on developing the aesthetic aspects of improvisation, especially on ballads.

Jazz Arranging II, which focuses on composing and arranging for the large ensemble, needed to be delayed until the fourth year to allow the student to acquire some stylistic maturity and to assimilate the techniques learned in Jazz Composition and Jazz Arranging I. The senior recital, which should be given as late as possible in the fourth year to allow maximum development, is obviously a course designed to give the student the opportunity to show the scope of what he/she has been able to assimilate and develop over the four-year period.

As for the course in Jazz Pedagogy, such a course should be taken only after all other jazz courses are completed or at least in progress, as much of Jazz Pedagogy will be reflective. After all, if the curriculum was worth studying for four years, and the results pleasing, then it also provides the best format for the pedagogy course, even though the student is invited to improve on that curriculum if he/she wishes, during the course, by designing one of his/her own. We each, as jazz educators, should mold the jazz curriculum to suit what we feel in our hearts to be the best way to serve and develop our students, whether it is as same as, or different from the manner in which we were taught. Furthermore, there are sometimes reasons why a curriculum may need to differ from one situation to another. There are different levels and lengths of study, as evident in secondary schools (high schools), junior colleges (2-year colleges), college/university 4-year programs, masters level, etc.. Some jazz programs will be within a department of music, some in a school of music, some in a liberal arts or fine arts program, each affecting curricula considerably. Then there are regional considerations, in that some areas are urban, some rural, some with very little community culture, others very sophisticated, some very very competitive or elite, others less so. Consequently, what is good for one situation may be ill-advised for another, or at least need considerable revision.

The Jazz Pedagogy course should, in addition to reflecting on the curriculum just taken, include a survey of books and other materials for each of the jazz courses, especially focusing on alternatives to the ones used in the courses taken at the institution they attended. Books on jazz pedagogy and directing jazz ensembles should also be surveyed. Each student should be given the opportunity to teach or present topics to the pedagogy class, receiving feedback from the instructor and the other class members for their efforts. The course should include jazz ensemble (large and small) directing and coaching techniques, as well as the opportunity to perform in that capacity for practice and feedback. Other topics might include a survey of announcements of graduate assistantships and positions in jazz (from the preceding year and the present time); how to prepare a resumè; collecting a notebook on all pedagogic materials (outlines, hand-outs, syllabi, publishers lists, curricula, etc.) that would be needed if the student should unexpectedly receive an opportunity to teach; practice in adjudicating ensembles at different levels of ability; learning to prepare clinics/lectures; becoming acquainted with the National Association of Jazz Educators and its journal; and examining brochures and curricula from other institutions.

Finally, with respect to the Jazz Pedagogy course, I require that my pedagogy students make individual appointments to 'invade' my office at a time when I am not in it. I'm well-organized and never keep anything in my office that is not needed for teaching, hence my office is filled with everything I need for teaching jazz (no more, no less). Therefore, my students benefit from taking notes on what is there, xeroxing and dubbing papers and tapes they think they might need for teaching, looking over tune collections, record and tape shelves, books, even hand-outs and examinations. I also provide them with a list of all the equipment and materials in my office (i.e., "258 color slides for Jazz History", "Kawai grand piano", "350 cassettes", "playback system", etc.), divided into two columns to show what has been provided for me by the department and what belongs to me personally (the latter being the longer list, by far!). I feel that their 'snooping' experience will alert them to what they need to ask for, should they be asked to start a jazz program somewhere or simply to teach in one, so that when the dean or department chairman asks them what they need for their new office, their list of needs will be more complete. I have found that if you need things for your new office, the best time to get action from the department, budgetarily speaking, is upon your arrival. They are generally more accomodating and agreeable at that time than they will likely be later, when your presence may be taken for granted, and it is generally presumed that if you survived last year without the items you might be requesting, then perhaps you don't really need it.

3

Teaching The Courses In The Jazz Curriculum

General Considerations

All jazz courses, with respect to the manner in which they are taught, will vary from individual to individual and from situation to situation. Being a highly creative musical style, there are as many approaches to teaching jazz courses as there are teachers. And this is good, as it affords the student a wide range of choices, and each teacher will be able to offer slightly different approaches to each subject. Not all students want, or respond to the same method, and so variety only increases the choices, from which each student can choose his/her favored way in which to approach the subject. Frequently, I encounter students who change schools, curricula, and teachers because they want a more complete spectrum of ways to study jazz. The teachers recognize these differences, too, and will sometimes suggest that the students might benefit more from study with a certain teacher at certain points within their development. For example, saxophonist/teacher David Liebman has sent students to me to get the 'nuts and bolts' of improvisation (chord/scales, theory, etc.), while I have sent students to Liebman who have needed a more intuitive approach to the subject. In a similar manner, David Baker and I have exchanged students, for still another set of reasons. Though Jamey Aebersold,

David Baker, and myself have been referred to as the 'ABC's of Improvisation', we recognize that each of us has a slightly different approach to the subject, and since each student also has varying notions about how they can best study the subject, they should have a choice and/or a recommendation from each of us. If I can learn, from each of my students, new ways to approach the subject (and I do), then the obvious conclusion is that there are too many details and too many approaches for any one person to claim total understanding or that further learning is not possible or necessary. The perpetually changing world of jazz is reason enough to continue searching, learning, and practicing. I have been teaching jazz for thirty-five years, yet my approaches to teaching the subjects of jazz are in a state of constant revision and renewal. Some of the changes are slight, such as selecting a few different tunes for improvisation classes, or adding a new handout for jazz piano class, or adding a small, new segment to the jazz pedagogy course. Some of the changes are more substantial, such as completely revising my approach to jazz arranging (new text, new syllabus, new assignments, etc.) almost overnight, or adding a new course, or assigning a different teacher to an already existing course. Whether the change is slight or substantial, however, I always feel that it was necessary and the program always seems to change for the better.

The Importance of the Ear

The most priceless musical attribute a teacher of jazz can possess, even more important than knowledge, is a well-developed ear. If you don't have that ability at present, then work on it, for the sake of your students. The musical ear can be developed, and anyone can improve their ears as much as they wish! It's a tedious task for some, but we all have an obligation to develop our ears as completely as we can, as it directly affects our teaching effectiveness. How can you solve an improviser's problems if you don't know (by listening alone) what specific pitches and rhythms were played? You could say "That sounds wrong", but you may not be correct, and even if you are, such a response is too unspecific to be of much help to the student. Had you perceived it completely, you might have been able to say "That's a G–7, not a G7, so don't forget to lower the third", or "That was a +4 you played there, which is a good note, but you need to learn how to use it better, perhaps by preceding the note and leaving it with better note choices", or "That phrase would have worked, but you fell behind one full measure, so that the change was already over." How can you check the accuracy of solos transcribed by a student for Analysis of Jazz styles class if you can't tell simply by listening? How can you catch copying errors on student arrangements if, when they are rehearsed, you can't look at the score while listening and know whether what you're seeing matches what you're hearing? How can you check the accuracy of voicings and progressions played by members of the jazz piano class (without having to move continuously around the room in order to look at their hands) if you can't hear them and know? And these same needs are also crucial to your effectiveness in conducting ensembles, teaching private lessons, listening to recitals (jazz), auditioning new students, evaluating students in proficiency examinations and end-of-term juries, etc.. You might wonder why teachers of classical music aren't required to have such well-developed ears (some are, and do!), but it's more crucial in jazz because you're hearing newly created music on a constant basis, in improvisation, arrangements, ensemble rhythm sections, etc., plus the fact that the harmonic progressions of jazz are subject to so many versions, substitutions, and reinterpretations.

Even your own development depends largely upon your ability to understand what you're hearing on record and what's going on around you in a playing situation, if you are to grow as a performer. Improvisation, put simply, involves (heavily) the ability to play what we hear! We can, and should, learn the theory, scales, progressions, patterns, licks, etc., but unless the ear is concurrently developed, the result will be cold, uninspired, mechanical, unoriginal, lacking in heart, beauty, spontaneity, and emotion. Remember, too, that if the development of the musical ear is important to you, as a performer and teacher, it is also important to each of your students. Though little is said about ear-training* in this book, within the sections on curriculum and syllabi, I nonetheless inject questions, projects, and examinations of the development of my student's ears throughout all the subjects of jazz.

Student Attitudes

The attitudes of our students have a great deal to do with their ability to learn, the rate of their development, their success-failure ratio, even their creative musical style. An initially poor student can progress rapidly if he/she has the right attitude toward self, teachers and friends, the school and the process of learning. Conversely, a very talented student with the wrong attitude can greatly impede his/her own progress, even fail via self-destruction. Because their attitudes are so crucial to their success or failure, both as a student and a professional (and as a person), it is very important for them to receive some assistance from their friends and teachers. For starters, our attitudes as teachers must not be the source of a bad attitude in any of our students. Furthermore, their bad attitude must not affect our attitude adversely. We must learn to transcend their poor demeanor if we are to be of any help...and we must! The longer I teach the more I find myself working on the attitudes of those around me(students and faculty), because I've come to know that virtually nothing will be accomplished until attitudes have been straightened and set on the right path. Even a passive, convictionless, or lazy attitude can be almost as negative as a

* All of side B of the tape that is sold with Vocal Improvisation: An Instrumental Approach (Patty Coker and David Baker) is devoted to several important approaches to ear-training, should the reader need specific materials for training self and students.

bad attitude, and most certainly must be addressed, also. For those with the latter problem, the remedy primarily lies in building self-confidence, drawing out their feelings and opinions, and helping them to establish practice habits, self-discipline, tenacity, and the joy of industry. Unfortunately, very few college-age people have been given the sort of upbringing they so desperately needed for their college education and life after graduation. I refer to such necessary things as the ability to work hard, the ability to organize their time, the ability to make and keep commitments, the ability to control their sleep/rest schedules and sexual urges, the ability to avoid and remedy physical illness (colds, allergies, influenza, etc.), knowledge about nutrition and the preparation of food, avoidance of drugs and alcohol, personal and environmental hygiene, and commitment to a spiritual path. The foregoing list may seem long and/or exaggerated to the reader, but a problem or lack with any one of the items on that list can greatly impede, even nullify, the student's chances for success! Add to that the fact that most of our students suffer a lack in several, even many, of those areas, and we are left wondering how they can be expected to survive, much less succeed. They're half-defeated before we begin to try to teach them about music! We may not be their parents, but unless we can influence their personal attitudes and disciplines, our ability to teach them about music will be limited even before we've begun to try. They must also be taught how to study and practice. Take a walk down the practice room corridors and you'll discover that many of our students are not there, or they're there but not playing, or they are only reviewing what they already know, or they're talking with another student, or they're incessantly repeating something that is incorrect, not solving problems, or simply inefficient. Practicing in itself is a skill. We probably need a course in that, too.

To help solve the problem, teachers would be wise to compose a few handouts which address some or all of the foregoing problems. We still need to talk to and deal with individuals, but such hand-outs might fall into the hands of students who have the problems but aren't discussing them with you. At the very least you'll be saving some lesson and class time by handing them something they can read on their own time. A few attitudinal papers have been included in the appendix of this book as samples for you to read. When trying to deal with the more hostile attitude, try to avoid being pulled down to their level of communication. Remember, a hostile attitude is very close to, perhaps even is, a form of mental illness, and the mentally ill most frequently turn on the ones they love most and those who love them the most. If you succumb to their seeming hostility, you can no longer help them. You eliminate yourself as their source of help in their time of need. We're not their parents and we're not psychiatrists, but we've all known parents and psychiatrists that were not of much help, either. We have to try. Love is always the answer.

Students also need to be alerted to how long their practice sessions might need to be. I recently polled the applied music faculty of the university where I teach, asking them to indicate, approximately, how much time per day they expected of their private students. The results were quite interesting. On the average, each expected the students to practice as many hours per day as the number of credit hours they were receiving for private lessons; that is, one hour per day for one hour of university credit, two hours per day for two hours credit, and so on. At our school, one credit indicates an elective student, often a non-music major, who receive one half-hour lesson per week. Everything above one hour credit is for music majors of one program or another, and they all receive one one-hour lesson per week, but the more hours they enroll for, the more is expected of them. Music Education majors enroll for two hours credit, Jazz and Woodwind majors enroll for three credits, and classical Performance majors enroll for four credits. According to this rule of measure, then, our jazz majors should be practicing at least three hours per day. I strongly suspect that only a few are doing so. Furthermore, the applied faculty indicated that they were conceiving this plan as a seven-day plan, not five, yet many students go home, attend out-of-town sporting events, have dates and/or attend parties, or simply rest on weekends. Also, a number of the faculty indicated that if the student is really serious about a career in professional music, they might need to increase considerably the number of hours they practice per day. I tell my students about some of the jazz legends and how much they practiced per day (eight hours for Sonny Stitt, five for Art Farmer, sometimes eleven for John Coltrane, etc.), but I never know whether or not they were affected by receiving that information. I also remind them that many of those players were genius or near genius level players, and that those of us who are not that gifted might need even more practice time. Finally, I assure them that if they are to become one of the jazz greats, they must not only enjoy practicing, but they need to become obsessed with practicing! Shortly after the survey was taken of the applied faculty, one of my Jazz Pedagogy students was giving a practicing lecture to the jazz majors, as part of an assignment. During the question and answer session, at the end of his lecture, a student asked him how much he thinks they should practice per day. To my horror he answered "About one and a half hours"! I realized that he had just informed me why his progress had been so marginal.

Listening Habits of Jazz Students

As it is for practicing, students need to be informed about how many hours per day they need to spend listening closely (not as background music, and not casual listening) to the many great artists on their many recordings. Again, most of the jazz greats logged many hours of listening (and at a higher perceptive level than our students, probably), both before and after they became prominent, successful, and influential. For example, both Michael Brecker and Dave Sanborn have gone on record as saying to young students/imitators that they wish the students would spend more time listening to the players they (Brecker and Sanborn) listened to, instead of restricting their listening and imitation to Brecker or Sanborn. For the students who are not even sufficiently attuned to jazz to know of players like Brecker and Sanborn (and there are a surprising number of those who come into a jazz program, usually because they were only listening to rock n'roll and pop music), the problem is much more critical. They cannot emulate what they have never heard! I am reminded of the early years of my teaching, when I frequently taught music theory courses in addition to jazz courses. I would ask my theory students how many of them owned more classical recordings than any other musical style. On the average, only one or two students out of thirty-forty would raise their hands, maybe three-four raising their hands for jazz, and the remainder responding to the rock n' roll call! Then I would look at my Walter Piston text, filled with its 'familiar' examples taken from classical music, and wonder just how familiar an augmented sixth chord from a Beethoven piano concerto was going to sound to them. And if it didn't sound familiar to them, how were they supposed to make the visual and aural connection the next time they saw or heard an augmented sixth chord? Many were the times, too, when instructing a saxophonist in classical music, I would quickly discover that they had never heard or heard of Marcel Mule, Sigurd Raschér, Eugene Rousseau, Larry Teal, or any of the saxophone quartets. Nor were they inspired by Bird, Rollins, or Trane. They simply played saxophone because their concert band/marching band director in high school assigned the instrument to them, and their musical experience was municipal park band music. I seriously doubt that they had any records of that music, either. In conclusion, we must remember that many, if not most, of our so-called students of jazz really don't know what their 'chosen' music even sounds like. They're once again going to need a lot of help, including recordings that go far beyond what might have been presented to them in a freshman level Jazz History course.

Teaching the Courses

At this point we need to turn to the specific approaches that can be taken with each of the jazz courses listed in the suggested curriculum contained in Chapter 2. A basic format will be used in the discussion of each subject:

(1) a syllabus for the course, also indicating a recommended text;
(2) suggestions and samples of needed hand-outs and supplements;
(3) a discussion of alternate possibilities for a text; and
(4) miscellaneous suggestions for teaching the course.

History of Jazz

Text: ***Listening to Jazz*** *(Coker)*

Week 1	Distribution of course syllabus. Statement of purpose, procedure, policy. Nature of examinations. Announcements regarding public jazz concerts and recitals and media (radio, TV) presentations. Brief performance by teacher. Listening and discussion of materials contained in Chapter 1 of text.
Weeks 2-3	Tape/slide presentation in the form of an accelerated overview of jazz history. Introduction to the song forms as contained in Chapter 2 of text, with in-class demonstrations of various song forms utilized by jazz performers. Listening and analysis of song forms on records, followed by a brief quiz on the same topic. In-class concert of the songs of Duke Ellington.
Weeks 4-6	Lecture/discussion of the functions of the rhythm section, as contained in Chapter 3 of text. Extensive listening to rhythm sections on record and the individual performers/soloists within them.
Week 7	Mid-term examination, covering material of Chapters 1-3 of text, with a review of the examination results in the meeting following the test.
Weeks 8-9	Lecture/demonstrations on the material of Chapter 4 (The Improvised Solo), including an introduction to the various vehicle-types, how the improviser prepares for each type, and a brief concert by the teacher, illustrating the vehicle-types in practice.
Weeks 11-13	Chapter 5 (Improviser's Hall of Fame) Extensive listening and guided analysis of solos by six of the best improvisers in jazz history. Presentation of video tape of

	Miles Davis (from N. E. T.).
Week 14	Review of jazz history via recordings. Preparation for final examination. Overviews and glossary.
Week 15	Final examination, to cover Chapters 4-5 only.

Hand-Outs/Supplements

Since most of the recordings played in class will come from the Smithsonian Collection, some students may wish to purchase same. In any event a listening list should be provided for all students taking the course.

Alternate or additional Text Possibility: ***Jazz Styles*** *(Mark Gridley)*

Additional Teaching Suggestions

The syllabus and text shown for this course is predicated on the fact that most of the students will be non-jazz and non-music majors. Therefore the focus is upon helping them to become interested in jazz music and become better listeners. It still serves the jazz major aurally, philosophically, and historically, though the terminology and level of musical intricacy is geared to avoid intimidation of the non-jazz, non-music major. Some programs, however, may choose to offer either a second section of the same course that is restricted to jazz majors, or have the jazz majors take the course along with the non-jazz, non-music majors, but offer them a more difficult course at some later point in the curriculum.

Jazz Theory

Text: ***The Jazz Theory Workbook*** *(Boling)*

I. Chord Structures (general)

A. Tertian
- (1) structured in third intervals (major and minor)
  - a) 1-3-5-7-9-11-13 (7 notes)
  - b) triads, seventh, etc.
    - 1) classical music uses mostly triads, V7, VIIo7, and secondary dominants (V7 of V, V7 of VI, etc.)
    - 2) triads are rare in jazz, leaning more toward extended chords (9ths, 11ths, 13ths, and altered chord notes)
  - c) 9 = 2
    11 = 4
    13 = 6
    9ths, 11ths, and 13ths are used in any combination; that is, for example, a 13th chord does not necessarily contain a 9th or an 11th.

B. Quartal
- (1) structured in fourth intervals (usually perfect fourth intervals)
  - a) generally stacked in groups of 3-5 notes;
    common examples: "So What" voicing and modal voicings.
  - b) quartal voicings occur most often in modal tunes.

C. Contemporary
structured with more seconds (major and minor), clusters, polychords, and chords with special bass tones (often used as pedal point).

II. Chord Structures (specific)

A. Tertian

as shown in Chord/Scale Compendium of Complete Method For Improvisation (Coker).

B. Quartal

(1) *So What* voicing

(2) left hand piano voicings (modal)

(3) chord-type applications;

i. e., -7, maj7, 7, 7sus.4, etc.

C. Contemporary

as used in compositions of Ron Miller, Herbie Hancock, John Surman, etc.

III. Chord/Scales

A. Chord/Scale Compendium (op. cit.)

B. Quartal (modal)

(1) pentatonic scales

(2) tetrads

(3) 4 + 2 intervals

(4) plus 7-note scales

C. Contemporary

(1) examples from Ron Miller, John Surman, etc.

(2) synthetic scales;

i. e., Treni (Embryo), Ron Miller (Wood Dance), Woody Shaw(Little Red's Fantasy, Katrina Ballerina, and others), David Liebman (Lookout Farm and others), etc.

IV. Chord Progressions (generally tertian)

A. General tendencies
   (1) cycle, chromatic, minor third, and major second motions.
   (2) common units (containing more than 2 chords)
      a) i. e.,II-V-I and extensions of same (such as #IV-VII-III-VI-II-V-I), I-IV7, turnarounds (or turnbacks), Confirmation sequence, Rhythm changes, Sears Roebuck bridge, and Montgomery Ward bridge.
   (3) common modulation patterns;
      as shown in Appendix D of *Improvising Jazz* (Coker)
   (4) common-tone scale sequences;
      i. e., *500 Miles High* (Corea)
   (5) CESH (Contrapuntal Elaboration of Static Harmony);
      as presented in *Jazz Keyboard*, Section 2 (Coker)
   (6) tendencies of rock/pop music;
      as shown in Farber

V. Bebop Scale

A. see hand-outs, taken from *How To Play Bebop* (Baker); surrounding tones (enclosures)

VI. Ear-Training (computer lab)

A. Chord/Scale indentification (no ear training)
B. Chord Quality recognition
C. Common Progression Units

Hand-Outs/Supplements

None needed, if Boling's book is used.

Alternate Text Possibilities:

The Jazz Language (*Dan Haerle*)

Jazz Theory (*Andrew Jaffe*)

Though not yet in print as of this date, The Jazz Theory Workbook by Mark Boling is likely to be the book that will satisfy the needs of the outline given here. Boling has team-taught the course with this author, we are in accord with respect to the objectives of the course, and the near-complete manuscript has been reviewed by this author.

Additional Teaching Suggestions

With the exception of Jazz History and Jazz Piano (classes), all other courses in the jazz curriculum presented in Chapter 2 are likely to be taken only by jazz majors, including Jazz Theory. Therefore, the objective of the course is to prepare jazz majors for the more penetrating subjects of the second, third, and fourth years, especially the improvisation courses. The nomenclature and symbology, then, need not be toned down to accomodate non-jazz and non-music-majors. They should be complete, realistic, and indicate alternate terminology used by other authors, teachers, and practitioners of jazz.

Though the definition and application of chord/scales might necessarily form the core of the course content, other aspects must not be ignored. For example, the jazz students need to be shown how chords function in a progression, common progression tendencies need to be assimilated, chord substitution principles learned, etc., and much of what is covered should be played by the students in class (though probably not improvised upon, the students assimilate facts better if they are involved with performing scales, chords, patterns, etc.).

Because the course contains a multitude of information, much of it is likely to be initially unfamiliar to the students, they should be given more frequent testing, in the form of brief quizzes, so as to avoid the confusion of one fact with another. And if their test performances are weak, then the students should be reviewed over the material and tested again. Unlike many courses, the goal of the Jazz Theory class needs to be 100% understanding, as opposed to simply achieving a passing score. After all, their later improvisations and arrangements cannot be successful if they are only 60% accurate! Art music is evaluated primarily on its artistic, aesthetic merit, with theoretical and technical accuracy being merely a prerequisite for creation.

Finally, because the ear plays such a crucial role in jazz performance, the ear-training aspects of the course are of utmost importance. Each and every new principle taken up should be heard often, played, and committed to the ear. Any theoretical principle that is merely discussed, even understood (in the mind), but not transferred to the ear, is not really learned and is relatively useless to the student. Remember, music is sound, and this definition especially affects the creative, spontaneous practitioner of jazz music.

Jazz Piano 1

Text: ***Jazz Keyboard*** *(Coker)*, pp. 1-36 and 41-51

Week 1 Distribution of syllabus. Discussion of purposes and activities of course. Explanation of 1st performance assignment, due at Week 2's meeting (all assignments will be explained in the week prior to their due date). Reading assignment: pp. 1-14 of text.

Week 2 Perform Exercise 1 (p. 11) in G, B♭, and D♭.

Week 3 Perform Figure 13 (p. 16) in 12 keys, playing only the II and V chords (omit the I chords). See Exercise 3, p. 19. We will explain and play Progression 1 ("Tune-Up") on p. 21 in class, though you needn't prepare it in advance, but do prepare Progressions 2 ("Pent-Up House") and 3 ("It's You Or No One") for Week 4.

Week 4 Perform Figure 24 (p. 25) in 12 keys, including the I chord. Progressions 2 and 3 will be played. Progressions 4 and 5 for Week 5.

Week 5 Perform Figure 23, p. 24 (II, V, I in minor). Progressions 4 (p. 22) and 5 (p. 26) will be played.

Week 6 Progressions 6 and 7 (no graded exercise/performance for this meeting). Explanation of rootless voicings and introduction to the blues (pp. 30-33). Prepare blues in G for Week 7.

Week 7 Perform blues in G (with minimal right-hand improvisation). Progressions 8 and 9 (p. 27) will be played also. Prepare blues in C, F, B♭, and E♭ for Week 8.

Week 8 Perform blues in C, F, B♭, and E♭. Progressions 10 and 11 (p. 28) will be played also. Explanation and assignment of CESH (pp. 41-45).

Week 9 Perform 3 CESH examples (your choice). Explanation and assignment of the dominant seventh chord with a suspended fourth. Prepare the sus. 4 chord (pp. 45-46) in 12 keys for Week 10.

Week 10 Perform sus. 4 chord in 4 keys (instructor's choice). Instructor will also provide several tunes to be played which utilize the sus. 4 chord extensively, for practice. Explanation and assignment of "So What" voicing (pp. 47-51).

Week 11 Perform tune (your choice), using only "So What" voicings, in a parallel fashion.

Week 12 Review of Progressions 1-5 with accompaniment tracks (warning: most tempos will be faster than previously played in class).

Week 13 Review of Progressions 6, 7, 10, and 11 with accompaniment tracks. Review of blues in C, F, B♭, and E♭ with accompaniment tracks.

Week 14 Play the tune you have selected to play on the final examination (1 - 7 - 3 - 5 voicings with added melody). This will not be graded, but is merely a chance to become accustomed to performing before others and to receive suggestions for improvement from the instructor.

Week 15 Final examination, consisting of prepared tune, 2 choruses of the blues in one of the 5 keys assigned previously (my choice), and sightreading of a progression.

Because Jazz Piano I and Jazz Piano II are sequential courses in the same subject, the syllabus for Jazz Piano II is presented next, without interruption, followed by the discussion of hand-outs, alternate text possibilities, and additional teaching suggestions that apply to both courses.

Jazz Piano II

Text: ***Jazz Keyboard** (Coker)*, pp. 37-41 and 51-57)

Week 1 Distribution of syllabus. Assign II - V - I progression in major, with rootless voicing, with 3rd on the bottom (Fig. 38, p. 37) in 12 keys. Also read pp. 37-40.

Week 2 Perform II - V - I (major, 3rd on bottom) in 12 keys. Prepare II - V - I (in major), with 7th on the bottom, in 12 keys (Fig. 38) for Week 3. Also, prepare Progression 1 ("Tune-Up", p. 21) for next meeting.

Week 3 Perform II - V - I (major, 7th on bottom) in 12 keys. Progression 1 will be played also. Prepare II - V - I in minor (3rd on bottom) in 12 keys (pp. 40-41) for Week 4, along with Progressions 2-4.

Week 4 Perform II - V - I (minor, 3rd on bottom) in 12 keys. Play Progressions 2-4. Prepare II - V - I (minor, 7th on bottom) in 12 keys for Week 5, along with Progressions 5-7.

Week 5 Perform II - V - I (minor, 7th on bottom) in 12 keys. Play Progressions 5-7. No assignment for Week 6 other than to prepare Progressions 8-11.

Week 6 Play Progressions 8-11. Distribution of hand-out with 2 blues comping exercises, to be performed at Week 7. Also, memorize and prepare first 2 Idiomatic Keyboard Vamps (IKV), "Watermelon Man" and "Cantaloupe Island" (p. 54).

Week 7 Perform 2 blues comping exercises, and be ready to play first 2 IKV's (from memory). Prepare blues with bass line (hand-out) and IKV's "All Blues" and "Killer Joe."

Week 8 Perform blues with bass line and play 2 assigned IKV's. Prepare "I Got Rhythm" comping (hand-out) and IKV's "Coral Keys" and "What Was" for Week 9.

Week 9 Perform "I Got Rhythm" comping and play 2 assigned IKV's. Introduce quartal voicings (pp. 51-52) and suggest ways to exercise. Prepare IKV's "What Was" and "Mahjong" for Week 10.

Week 10 Practice quartal voicings (with side-slipping) with accompaniment tapes. Play two assigned IKV's. Prepare other keys for quartal voicings/improvisation, plus IKV's "Maiden Voyage" and "Nica's Dream" (on supplementary hand-out) for Week 11.

Week 11 Practice other keys with quartal voicings and play two assigned IKV's. Prepare "Reach Out" and "Senor Blues" (IKV's) for next time.

Week 12 Play 2 assigned IKV's. Discuss "Contemporary Chord Symbols" (pp. 52-53). Prepare "Wood Dance" and "Como en Vietnam" for next time.

Week 13 Play last 2 IKV's and review all 14 IKV's. Prepare tune selected (your choice) for final examination (rootless voicings, plus melody).

Week 14 Play selected tune for instructor and class (not for grade). Discuss final.

Week 15 Final exam, consisting of prepared tune, quartal (modal) improvisation, about 4 of the 14 IKV's (my choice), either "Blues With Bass Line" or "I Got Rhythm" (your choice), and sight-reading (rootless, lefthand only).

Hand-Outs/Supplements

(1) Titles and melodies to the eleven tune progressions contained in text.

(2) Preferred inversions for the blues in each of the five assigned keys.

(3) A few known progressions which use the suspended fourth chord

exclusively.

(4) Some bass and drum tracks from play-alongs, on tape, to be used in class, on the blues, sus. 4 tunes, II-V and II-V-I exercises in twelve keys from the Aebersold series, the eleven progressions used in the text, and some modal tune tracks.

(5) A hand-out explaining how to arrange the 1-7-3-5 voicings (Jazz Piano I) so as to be able to perform both chords and melodies on the eleven tunes in the text.

(6) Additional Idiomatic Keyboard Vamps (see end of Section 3 of text).

(7) Optional: expanded uses of the "So What" voicing, "I Got Rhythm" study/voicings with tri-tone substitutions in bridge, more contemporary voicings, and bass lines (walking) for the left hand.

Alternate Text Possibilities

Though there exists a large number of books published for jazz piano, actually none of them address the specific needs of this course (yet, anyway) besides the text shown on the two syllabi. Nearly all of them are written expressly for pianists excluding non-pianists who need to learn to use the keyboard. Consequently, most of the other texts would be too demanding for the non-pianist, leaving out the sort of techniques and methods that produce the quick results that are needed at this level. Nevertheless, other books that might serve as excellent supplements, or service a jazz piano course for pianists would include:

Jazz/Rock Voicings For The Contemporary Keyboard Player *(Dan Haerle)*

Transcribed Piano Voicings *(Jamey Aebersold)*

From A New Approach To Jazz Improvisation, Vol. 1

Additional Teaching Suggestions

Be prepared for the student who is intimidated by the piano. Perhaps it is better that a non-pianist teaches the course, to alleviate some of the fear shared by many non-pianists in the course. Don't lose too much time teaching posture, fingerings, tone, reading (notation), finger speed, and other topics that serve pianists more than non-pianists. Make it seem easy. Be patient. Don't be surprised if, at first, they can only perform the exercises by working out a system of watching their hands and "moving this finger here and that finger there", instead of actually being aware of the identity of each chord, key, note-of-chord, etc. That will come later, when their minds catch up with their fingers, but first they need to be able to play and build some confidence.

Though the course is primarily designed for non-pianists, it will be found that the course will probably fill gaps and help the freshmen jazz pianists to a considerable degree. And the pianists who are not jazz majors certainly won't be getting the information contained in this course from their classical piano teachers, so don't expect them to become bored or cause the non-pianists to feel foolish.

When writing voicings on the chalkboard, get in the habit of using letters instead of conventional notation. It gets the job done and doesn't intimidate the students who read notation poorly, or have difficulty with reading both clefs.

Example:

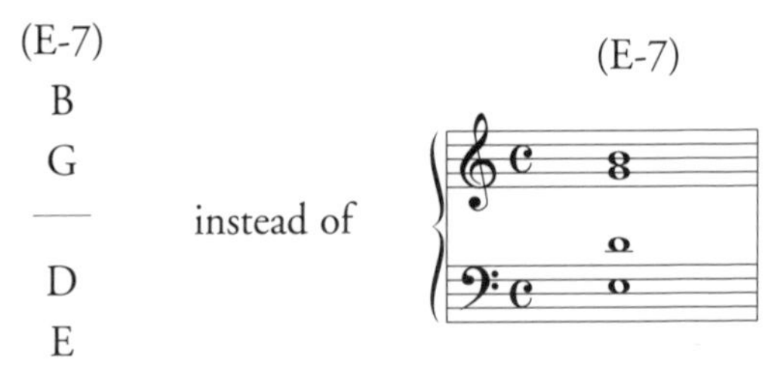

Jazz Improvisation I

Text: ***Complete Method For Improvisation*** *(Coker)*
(Chapters 1-3)

Week 1 — Distribution of syllabus. Bring instruments/amps to all future meetings. Distribution of hand-outs (5). Determine instrument keys for all class members to facilitate tune hand-outs for second meeting, and take orders for all play-alongs needed for course. Begin playing scales (pp. 9-10) and digital patterns (hand-out) at second meeting. Begin preparing "Essential Patterns and Licks" (hand-out) for Week 2. Read pp. 3-10 in text.

Week 2 — Apply digital patterns and "Essential Patterns" (1-4) to exercise tracks of play-alongs, "Giant Steps" and other tunes. This procedure will continue for several weeks, until patterns 1-17 are covered.

Weeks 3-7 — Continuance of pattern practice and application. Perform melodies and improvise on all assigned Bebop and Standard vehicles (on handouts and practice tape). Learn and apply 7th-3rd resolution on II-V progression (pp. 29-33). Read pp. 11-46 in text.

Week 8 — Playing examination on bebop tune, plus a written midterm examination.

Weeks 9-11 — Modal tunes. "Aural Familiarization With All Scale Tones" (pp. 56-57). Pentatonic scales and fourth intervals (pp. 49-50, 62, and hand-out). Intensity-building devices (pp. 60-61). Melodic development (pp. 57-60). Side-Slipping/Outside Playing (pp. 62-64). Perform melodies and improvise on all assigned modal tunes (hand-outs and tape). Read Chapter 2 (pp. 47-65).

Weeks 12-14 — The Blues. Read Chapter 3 (pp. 66-74). Perform all

	assigned blues tunes. Listening to good 'models' on record. Emphasis on uniqueness (p. 66), structure (67-70), and style (pp. 70-71, plus in-class listening).
Week 15	Playing examination on modal and blues vehicles, plus a written final examination.

Jazz Improvisation II

Texts: ***Complete Method For Improvisation*** *(Coker)*
(Chapters 4-6)
The Music of Ron Miller *(Miller)*

Week 1	Distribution of syllabus. Be sure to obtain Miller text in the key of your instrument. Read Chapter 4 (The Contemporary Vehicle, pp. 75-83). Learn the lydian-augmented scale and its 5 applications (pp. 35-39), plus "Modes and Applications of the Ascending Melodic Minor Scale" hand-out). Begin applying scale and "Cry Me A River" lick to II-V-I in minor. Distribute hand-out tunes for course.
Weeks 2-7	Play all tunes in Ron Miller play-along, plus other contemporary tunes on play-along provided by instructor.
Week 8	Playing examination on a contemporary tune, selected by instructor.
Weeks 9-12	The Ballad Vehicle (Ch. 5, pp. 84-86). Hand-outs on "Pretty: A Musical Definition of the Word" (with demonstrations by instructor) and "Ballad Playing." Playing of 5 selected ballads (on hand-outs and play-alongs), with emphasis on improvisational aesthetics.
Weeks 13-14	The Free Form Vehicle (Ch. 6, pp. 87-91. Practicing of extra-musical devices (p. 88). Listening to examples on record. Playing of student designed free form "compositions."
Week 15	Written final examiation.

Hand-Outs/Supplements (for both Improvisation I and II)

Lead lines and progressions for all tunes to be played in course, given to the students at the beginning of the courses, so that they can work ahead of the class activity at times. The provided lead sheets are in the key of their instrument.

Play-alongs for all tunes to be used in course, so students can practice improvising before and between meetings of the class. Attitude-setting material (see sample, Requirements For Becoming a Good Jazz Improviser, on following pages).

Patterns (see Essential Jazz Patterns and Licks, on following pages).

Alternate Text Possibility:

Creative Jazz Improvisation *(Scott Reeves)*

There are many other books on improvisation, including others by this author, but when a teacher selects a text, some emphasis needs to be placed on the book's suitability for day-to-day sequencing. Otherwise, even a very fine book (such as Baker's ***Jazz Improvisation*** and ***Advanced Improvisation***, Russell's ***Lydian Chromatic Concept***, Aebersold's ***A New Approach to Jazz Improvisation***, and Coker's ***Improvising Jazz*** or ***Patterns for Jazz***) are really more suitable as 'roll up your sleeves and play' methods, rather than texts.

Additional Teaching Suggestions

Don't succumb to making this course a course heavily-loaden with lectures. The students have a text, copies of all the tunes, and play-alongs for all of the tunes. They've taken a course in Jazz Theory, so there is no need to lecture excessively, especially about theoretical substance. Plan to have them play as much of the time as possible, only interrupting to give them feedback on their solos and to demonstrate certain points for them on your instrument. It's a good idea for the instructor to play the first solo of each 'round'. This gives them time to prepare for their solos, gives their ears a more-experienced interpretation before their solos, and often answers questions they might have had, and in a very efficient way. You may also want to play the original recording of as many of the tunes as possible, unless it seems to be reducing unduly the amount of student playing time needed (The recordings could be placed in the music library, to be listened to by the students on their own time).

This author has found that play-alongs, even with the disadvantages, are preferable to using too much class time trying to teach beginning rhythm section players how to play the accompaniment accurately, reliably, and with good taste. In other words, it should be taught as a melodic improvisation class (solo improvisation), rather than group concept. The latter can be focused upon during ensemble rehearsals, private lessons (for the pianists, guitarists, bassists, and drummers), and rhythm section clinics or courses. This means that the improvisation class' pianists and guitarists are not comping, the bassists are not playing walking lines, and drummers should play piano or vibraphones.

Plan to let each student play each tune twice, perhaps on different days, as it will be discovered that everyone tends to improvise about twice as well on the second try. Also, while the tune is in its first 'round' (the initial playing), it might be advisable to keep the solos short, to allow listening and recuperation time between efforts, lengthening the solos to more choruses as they seem ready for them. Along the same lines, it's helpful to the students, when playing fast-moving, difficult progressions, to have them alternate in two, four, or eight-measure segments, so they can focus on smaller units for awhile.

Use play-along exercise tracks while the class warms up on patterns at the beginning of class, so that they are constantly given the opportunity to make the aural association between a pattern and the chord that accompanies it. Warm up to the tunes by playing the patterns wherever possible, also. Patterns have to be ingrained if they are to occur to the player as an option during his/her solo. Even if the pattern is not used during the solo, at least the student will be hearing (mentally) something that could work.

Don't be alarmed if some of the students lose or gain beats and measures here and there. It's a common problem at first, but fades away quickly without making an issue of it. Just be ready to point to the right place, in case the problem arises, without interrupting the proceedings.

In rendering feedback to individuals, with regard to their solos, be gentle and kind, always offer solutions, remember to compliment them when they solve the problem, expect more of the better players, and when a better player plays something especially choice, clever, or resourceful, share it with the rest of the class by explaining it to them. For the first few weeks of the course (at least), focus on any and all inaccuracies and correct them quickly, so that each student quickly comes to know that wrong notes are audible, that you hear them (precisely), and that they are ultimately unacceptable. After a few weeks, they will come to know that there is no point in trying to bluff their way through something they haven't practiced. The problem stems from the fact that they can't yet hear the difference beetween right and wrong notes, and so they naturally presume that it is unlikely that anyone else hears or cares. Of course this sort of feedback has to continue indefinitely, though less pronounced, as each new harmonic or scalar sound will tempt them to try to bluff their way through again, for the same reasons. Often a new chord or scale quality (such as diminished, augmented, whole-tone, phrygian, or synthetic scales) will simply sound strange or wierd to the uninitiated ear, and so they may get the notion that anything they choose to play that is 'strange or wierd' will suffice, and no one will be the wiser. After they've played it correctly for awhile, however, they won't accept wrong notes either. Many will try to justify their mistakes, saying that it was a deliberate plan to play 'outside' or 'be more chromatic'. In time they'll get their chance to do things like that, even be urged by the instructor to do so, but by then they'll have a better idea as to how to execute it effectively, and where and when it would be most effective.

Requirements For Becoming a Good Jazz Improvisor

(1) **A Strong Desire.**

You must be more than mildly interested to succeed. At some point, perhaps even from the outset, the desire to improvise well should be obsessive!

(2) **Attunement To Style.**

Listen to and assimilate the best of jazz on record, old and new. Listen hard and repeatedly! Attend live performances, ranging from the jazz recitals of your classmates to concerts by touring jazz greats. You cannot improvise in a vacuum.

(3) **Will.**

The human will can accomplish anything! If you fail to utilize the will, you risk accomplishing nothing. The will is responsible for such characteristics as perseverance, patience, and consistency.

(4) **Energy.**

All music should contain some type of energy in performance. Energy levels are affected by life-style, attitude, nutrition, health, and a careful ordering of priorities.

(5) **Method.**

You must have a plan, if you are to reach your goals. The plan should be reasonable, efficient, and thorough.

(6) **Theory Understood.**

The mind must thoroughly unterstand each musical principle undertaken.

(7) **Theory Applied.**

Any theory understood in the mind but left unapplied is not learned, it will not appear in your improvisations, and it will soon be forgotten. In order for a theoretical principle to become useful, the mental unterstanding must be transferred and/or extended to the ears and hands.

(8) **Theory Challenged And Mastered.**

Work toward speed, accuracy, control, and flexibility of all theoretical principles, patterns, licks, scales, keys, etc.

(9) **Theory Utilized.**

Exaggerate the use of all new items by practicing them with appropriate play-along exercises (not tunes), but simulate creative performance mannerisms as well.

(10) **Theory Utilized In Consummate Creativity.**

Play many appropriate tunes which contain exaggerated use of harmonies which accommodate the theoretical principles taken up.

Essential Patterns And Licks

It has often been the case that students of improvisation will learn the theoretical aspects of the subject, but are prone to sounding simplistic, academic, sometimes aimless, with a noticeable absence of what David Baker has termed 'the language of jazz'... those patterns and licks which are continually shared by virtually all the great improvisers, as a part of the content of their solos. In other words, a reasonable percentage of most solos will and should contain familiar jazz phrases, as they are an essential means of musical communication. All of the patterns and licks shown in this study are extremely commonplace, yet effective and needed by all.

Be sure to practive each pattern/lick in every possible way, as such practice will ingrain the phrase into the fingers, ears, mind, and memory. Play the lick in all keys, using different modulation patterns (chromatic, cycle, etc.). Can it be altered slightly to enable it to fit different harmonic situations? Does it sound well when played from a different note of the chord? Is it effective when played backwards (retrograde)? If it is an ascending contour, is there a descending possibility (and vice versa)? Can it be connected smoothly to another pattern? Can it become a double-time pattern, if need be? Does it have potential for sequences or side-slips?

The process of ingraining is extremely important. An insufficiently-ingrained lick will not occur to you in the 'heat of battle', and even if it did, you'd probably be afraid to try it, because of the high risk of errors. Therefore it would be wise to follow the format given here to insure ingraining:

(1) practice pattern/lick, alone, without accompaniment (all keys, sequences, permutations, etc.);
(2) play pattern/lick (only) against an appropriate play-along exercise (i.e., a track from Aebersold's Volume 1, 3, 16, 21, etc., not a tune);

(3) improvise against the exercise track, but lean toward rather frequent use of the pattern/lick;
(4) practice the pattern/lick against a play-along tune that is harmonically appropriate for many applications of that phrase (i.e., Baker's "Le Miroir Noir" in JA-10, for applying diminished scale), using only the pattern/lick whenever possible; and
(5) improvise against a play-along tune, but exaggerate your use of the lick (you can moderate its use, once it is sufficiently ingrained). Look for other play-along tunes to which the pattern/lick may be applied. If you have an adjustable speed on your tape machine, play the tune(s) in other keys, to maximize your experience with playing the phrase.

Remember that you're trying to achieve a balance between the familiar (patterns/licks) and the unfamiliar (new and/or original ideas). Learning and ingraining these licks will not stifle your creativity. It will lend communication to your solos, and serve as springboards to original ideas. Your creativity will only be stifled if you never play anything original. The one thing you cannot afford to do is to operate in a stylistic vacuum.

Essential Patterns And Licks

A. Digital Patterns

Essential Patterns And Licks

D. I-VI7 Licks

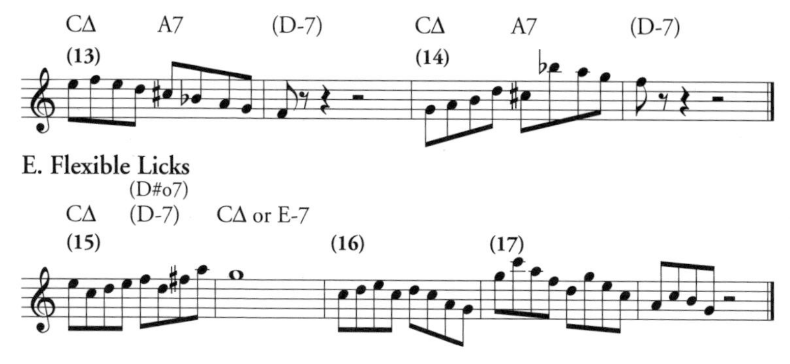

E. Flexible Licks

F. Diminished Patterns

G. Augmented Patterns

Analysis of Jazz Styles

Texts: ***28 Modern Jazz Trumpet Solos*** *(Slone)*
Modern Jazz Tenor Solos *(Butler)*

Weeks 1 - 2	Discussion of purpose and activities of course. Lecture on the functions and potential of the ear in music, taken from Chapter 2 of *The Jazz Idiom* (Coker).
Weeks 3 - 4	Survey of methods - techniques for transcribing solos, analytical techniques, and needed nomenclature, taken from The Jazz Idiom, Giants of Jazz series (Baker), and instructor's notes. Discussion of "Devices Commonly Found In Jazz Solos" (Coker), a hand-out. In-class solo transcription by entire class and instructor (bring instruments to class on that day).
Weeks 5 - 7	In-class listening to, and analysis of, first 10 solos (approximately) in texts.
Week 8	First transcription and analysis (by student) due.
Weeks 9 - 12	Listening and analysis of remainder of solos in Slone and Butler.
Weeks 13 -14	Listening and analysis of non-trumpet and non-tenor-solos, provided by instructor. Second transcription/analysis due on last day of 14th week (2 solos, with comparitive analysis)
Weeks 15	Return 2nd transcription/analysis papers to students. Written final examination last day.

Hand-outs/Supplements

List of the devices to be cited in analysis (see Devices Commonly Found In Improvised Solos, on succeeding pages).

Alternate Text Possibilities:

Any good collection of transcribed solos, of which there are far too many to list here. This author prefers collections which are of more than one artist, both to promote variety as to show commonality between all players.

Additional Teaching Suggestions

Most of the members of an Analysis of Jazz Styles class are not sure they can transcribe a solo. To combat their apprehension, this author likes to first work on their confidence to do the work, by reading certain passages from *The Jazz Idiom* (Coker), namely a treatise on the potential of the ear, contained in Chapter 2. Such a reading and discussion seems to make them more aware of the almost infinite (well beyond what they need to transcribe a solo) potential for the ear's development. Next comes a collectively-done transcription in class, with horns in hand, which affords the instructor the opportunity to help them to understand the techniques, objectives, and short-cuts in transcribing solos. Finally, they should be told that the choice of solo and player is up to them, as well as the length they choose to tackle. This gives them the flexibility to select solos that are accessible to their level of development. Most should probably start by transcribing players of their instrument, to take advantage of that instrumental attunement, as well as selecting players that might have drawn them to the instrument, initially, and might still be exerting considerable influence on their style.

Early in the course, also, should be a study of transcribing techniques and analytical techniques suggested by various authors. Then the devices common to all players (see following pages) should be discussed thoroughly, to be sure everyone understands and can recognize each device.

An interesting phenomenon takes place as the course progresses into listening to solos from the text and citing all occurrences of the common devices. At first the students tend to glean all their information by reading their copies of the solos (even that is difficult for some), but after awhile, they're hardly reading at all, because their ears begin to perceive the devices before their eyes and mind can decipher the written version!

Also, as the course progresses, the commonly-used devices are so prevalent that there is very little left unmarked in each of the solos, which convinces the students that the list of devices is indeed a capsulization of what is commonly referred to as 'the language of jazz' At the end of the course, they should be urged to examine the list again to determine how many of those devices have, as yet, become a part of their own improvisational style.

Devices Commonly Found In Improvised Solos

Analysis of Jazz Styles

Bebop Scale - the adding of a chromatic step to an otherwise 7-note scale, in order to align metric accents. In major scales the chromatic step occurs between the 5th and 6th degrees, in dorian scales it occurs between the 3 and 4, and between the 7th and root of mixolydian scales.

Bebop Lick - very closely related to the *bebop scale* (see above), in that it involves the same added chromatic step. However, the *bebop lick* is also a very specific melody. The bebop lick on a C7 chord, for example (also a G-7 chord), would be 'c-b-b♭-d-a-g'. Less frequently it also appears with a 'c' or an 'f' in place of the 'd'.

Enclosure (also referred to as **Surrounding Tones**) - an 'object tone' (consonant member of a chord or scale) approached first from a semi-tone above, then a semi-tone below, then the object tone (similar to upper and lower 'neighboring tones'). Example: an object tone of 'c' appearing in an enclosure would result in a 3-tone series of 'd♭-b-c'.

Blues Scale - (structure: 1, ♭3, 4, #4, 5, ♭7) though specifically developed for use in the conventional 12-bar blues, some players will use only sporadically in the blues (plus the fact that some blues progressions are less than wholly traditional), and players will frequently use the blues scale in a non-blues tune. It is one of the scales frequently chosen for *harmonic generalization* (see below).

Harmonic Generalization - the practice of lumping together several chords (especially closely-related chords, like II-V-I) with one scale. The major scale and the blues scale are most commonly used for this purpose, but scales like harmonic minor and diminished can be expected as well, along with still other possibilities.

Change-Running - the practice of arpeggiating the individual chords of a progression in improvisation, so that little else is occuring (such as definable melodies). A fast harmonic rhythm is usually the reason for such practice, and one can generally expect to find a consistent rhythmic level of 8th notes. Scales can also be a part of change-running.

Digital Patterns - closely related to change-running, digital patterns are small (usually 4-8 notes), well-organized notegroups such as 1-2-3-1, 1-2-3-5, 1-3-5-3, which are used to realize fast-moving chord progressions by transposing the patterns to fit each passing chord. Such patterns are usually practiced aside from and before actual performance.

Pentatonic Scales - (structure: 1,2,3,5,6 of a major scale) most commonly found in modal and blues tunes, but also found with less frequency in other situations. Uncommonly long phrases are often generated by the use of a single pentatonic scale. Side-slips (see below) are often based on pentatonics.

Side-Slipping (or **Outside Playing**) - the practice of deliberately leaving the given key, momentarily, and returning. Often the side-slip is to a key or chord that is a half-step higher than the given one, and pentatonic scales are often present. The device is used to create tension and avoid monotony.

Unusual or Substitute Scales - under the heading of *unusual scales* might be synthetic scales (originally-devised). Less-common modal scales (i.e. phrygian or locrian), harmonic major, gypsy minor, hindu scales, and all symmetrical scales (chromatic, whole-tone, diminished, augmented). Sometimes a player will substitute one of these scales (or another equally unusual one) for a much simpler, more traditional one.

Resolution of 7th to 3rd - refers to the common resolution of the seventh of a -7 chord (like II) to the 3rd of a 7 chord (like V) whose root is a fourth higher (or a fifth lower). For example, the resolution of 'c' to 'b' in a D-7 to G7 progression. Frequently this resolution is present in the melodies and patterns of an improviser.

CESH (Contrapuntal Elaboration of Static Harmony) - a harmonic device in which a chord of long duration has one moving voice to create interest, such as a long-running minor chord in which the root descends in half steps, but the other parts of the chord remain in place. Numerous melodies and patterns have been based on this harmonic device, and frequently a player will superimpose a CESH melody or pattern over a non-CESH harmony, especially II-V progressions and tonic (I) minor chords.

Tri-Tone Substitution - a harmonic substitution of a chord or chords which are a tri-tone (3 whole steps, or an augmented 4th, or a diminished 5th) away from the given chord, such as substituting D♭7 for a G7, or even A♭-7 D♭7 for D-7 G7. An Improviser does not necessarily wait for the subsitution to be present in the accompaniment before using it.

Leaps from the 3rd to a ♭9th - melodically, it is extremely common for an improvisor to play the 3rd of a dominant seventh chord, then move directly or indirectly (by including the 5th and/or 7th en route) to the lowered 9th. Such motion permeates much of the linear substance of a solo, especially on VI7 chords, and one will find about as many instances of the 3rd moving *down* (3 half steps down) to the lowered 9th as the instances in which an upward motion is used.

"Cry Me A River" Lick - a phrase which derives from a standard tune of the same name. In its original context, the melody descended as follows: 9, 8(1), 5, ♭3, 2, 1 (over a tonic minor chord). Although improvisers use the phrase in this same setting sometimes, it is even more common to find them using the same melodic intervals in a different harmonic setting, as follows: +9, ♭9, +5, 3, +9, ♭9 (still descending) over a dominant seventh chord with an augmented 5th and augmented 9th added.

"Gone But Not Forgotten" Lick - like the "Cry me a River" lick, a phrase which derives from a standard tune of the same name ("Gone But Not Forgotten"). It is nearly always used over a minor chord, using the digital formula, 9 (or 2) - ♭3 - #7 - 9 - 1 - 5. Example: against C–, the phrase would be 'd-e♭-b-d-c-g'.

Angularity - the use of uncommonly wide intervals in improvisation, very pronounced in players like John Coltrane, Eric Dolphy, Thelonious Monk, Woody Shaw, Benny Wallace, etc.

Sequences - re-use of same or similar pattern or melody over several successive changes of harmony.

Quotes - melodic fragments of other tunes or solos, woven into an improvisation, sometimes as a humorous touch, sometimes simply because the improviser hears that the quote is based on the same harmonic setting as what he presently faces. In a few instances, players have used quotes to be programmatic or to make a socio-political comment.

Shifting of Bar Line - The delaying or anticipating of the harmonic or rhythm progress (especially the former) so that it is occuring (seemingly) in the wrong place. It is a deliberate (usually) and temporary distortion of the meter and/or bar structure.

Inadvertent Repetition - the unintentional reiteration of a phrase within the same solo, often occuring at the same spot within a successive chorus or repeated section (and nearly always on the same chord root and chord-type), therefore separated from its first occurrence by a considerable length of time. If the phrase is reiterated *immediately* after the first occurrence, then it is probably deliberate rather than accidental. Inadvertent repetition usually indicates that the phrase is a personal cliché; or simply reinforces the notion that all players are prone to hearing the same phrase at certain points within the tune's progression (a natural aural phenomenon).

Error - an obvious mistake on the part of the improviser, yet dangerous for the inexperienced student analyzer to cite. If the given chord, for example, is C–, and the player plays an e-natural, or the chord is a C 7 and the player plays a b-natural, it is relatively safe to assume an error. However, the analyzer must also consider other possibilities first, such as substitute chords, bar-line shifts, or 'blue notes' (♭3, ♭5, or ♭7), for example. It could even be a side-slip (or outside playing). In any event, be cautious about labelling a suspected error, then look for possible causes, such as split notes, hitting wrong harmonics on a brass instrument, memory lapses, getting finger-tied, forgetting to repeat a section, etc., all of which can happen to anyone, which in itself is a lesson to the analyzer.

Jazz Composition And Arranging

Text: ***Jazz Arranging and Composing*** *(Dobbins)*

Weeks 1-2	Rhythmic rewriting of various types of melodies.
Weeks 3-4	Study of and listening to "46 Great Tunes" (instructor's collection). Notation and calligraphy.
Weeks 5-6	Re-harmonization techniques and techniques of chord substitution. Common aspects of chord progressions (drawn from Appendix D of Coker's *Improvising Jazz*). Begin composing tunes.
Weeks 7-8	Composing and in-class performances of original tunes (graded).
Weeks 9-11	(approx.) Study of small ensemble arranging (Dobbins), with short arranging assignments for various instrumentation.
Weeks 12-15	Original compositions/arrangements by students, to be played in class.

Hand-outs/Supplements

Lead lines (melodies) of standard tunes which are in need of rhythmic rewriting, for the purpose of adding syncopations and a more spontaneous sort of rhythmic phrasing.

Copies of choice tunes to be studied and analyzed for attributes. Hand-outs pertaining to reharmonization and chord substitution methods.

Hand-out listing harmonic and melodic aspects of tunes that cause them to be attractive to the listener.

Alternate Text Possibilities:

Arranging And Composing For The Small Jazz Ensemble *(Baker)*

Additional Teaching Suggestions

If students are to learn to tap their creativity and write attractive tunes, they must first be taught to learn more tunes, be exposed to great tunes they've never heard and/or analyzed and be shown what made the tunes successful, learn how to write effective progressions and melodies, and practice composing different kinds of tunes (standard, bebop, modal, blues, contemporary, etc.). In addition to studying the best tunes provided by the instructor, each student should be asked to produce a tape of some of their currently favorite tunes and state why they feel that each is a good tune, being careful not to confuse performer or arrangement with the tune itself (a great tune can be performed badly and a mediocre or weak tune, with a good arrangement and/or performance can sound deceptively good).

With respect to arranging a tune, the student should be made aware of the options they have, with regard to writing for 2-5 voices (unisons, octaves, thirds, sixths, fourths, stacked, open, drop 2, etc.), the various textures possible (homophonic, contrapuntal, harmonization, etc.), and ways to accomodate chromaticism in the melody. Keep the assignments short at first, so that the students have more time to do a better job with it, so that their assignments won't require as much time to play and tape, and so they won't risk the possibility of laboring over a long assignment only to discover that it was all done incorrectly. The assignments can be lengthened later, when the students are more 'on track'.

If the students are knowledgeable about MIDI and the university has the facilities, much class time can be saved if the students prepared their assignments on MIDI rather than having to read, rehearse, and tape them in class.

Be rather strict about the mechanics of arranging, especially at first, such as the quality of the calligraphy, accuracy of transposition for B♭ and E♭ instruments (including the correct octave), numbers of beats in measures, and other basic skills that pertain to the mechanical preparation of scores and parts. As it was mentioned about beginning improvisers who need to understand that wrong notes are unacceptable, and jazz theory students who need to think in terms of 100% accuracy instead of a passing score, it is also true that young arrangers need to understand the gravity of accuracy in the score and parts.

Many good, even great arrangements have been refused by professional ensembles simply because the parts were inaccurate, unnecessarily complicated (i.e., the inflated use of repeat signs, repeated measures, multiple D.S. and D.C. markings, 3rd and 4th endings, and verbalized short-cuts, like "play same changes as letter A and B, but play an A♭7 instead of the D♭–7 in the third bar, and use the 3rd ending only"), or simply because the parts were, for calligraphic reasons, hard to read. The student must be made to understand that they must produce scores and parts which practically 'read themselves'. Joseph A. Artis, who was my teacher of classical piano, theory, and arranging when I was fifteen years old, used to say (repeatedly), "Remember, you are always responsible for the other fellow's mistakes"! While his memory is once again revived, let me add another axiom he used to repeat often to composers and arrangers, this time relating to what they might be chosing to write in their scores. He would say, "What does not sound well should not be written"! It's easy to see why the memory of him lingers for a lifetime, for those who were fortunate enough to study with him. His axioms, and there were many, were simple, true, and forever valid and helpful.

When arranging students ask for assistance or feedback from you, don't simply tell them what you think they ought to do, as you want to protect their creativity somewhat, rather than create a clone of yourself. On the other hand, don't send them away to re-do the assignment without any new input from you. The best thing you can do for them is to trigger their own creativity by mentioning a host of options they may have overlooked, options which could be combined, and solutions that were used by well-known composers/arrangers on recordings they've heard. By merely triggering their innate creativity they may come back with yet another solution, one that is equal or better than what you might have done, better than any one of the options you mentioned, even better than what the well-known person recorded.

For teaching melodic form, this author uses excerpts from *Jazz Improvisation* (David Baker), or *Arranging And Composing For The Small Jazz Ensemble* (Baker), and *Improvising Jazz* (Coker), all of which contain segments on melodic development.

Jazz Arranging II

Text: ***Inside The Score*** *(Wright)*

Weeks 1-5 (approx.) Study of the scores and large ensemble writing techniques of Nestico, Jones, and Brookmeyer (text).

Weeks 6-10 (approx.) Study of the Clare Fischer scores on "Extensions" (provided by instructor). Study (through listening) of other arrangers, to include Charles Mingus, Gil Evans, Ron Miller, and Coker.

Weeks 11-15 (approx.) Students select tunes, submit 'plans', write scores, and copy parts for arrangements for large jazz ensemble, to be played and taped by the Jazz Ensemble.

Hand-outs/Supplements

In this author's course, students are given copies of the scores from the album, *Extensions*, by Clare Fischer. Fischer's genius as a composer/arranger (especially in the area of harmonies and voicings) are well-known to some of us who write music (Herbie Hancock and Bill Dobbins, for starters!). Because of a long, enduring friendship, this author was fortunate enough to have received copies of *Extensions*, which, by the composer's own testimony, was some of his finest work. So it was only natural that this material be placed in the hands of young arrangers who could benefit from the many revelatory aspects of Fischer's mastery of the idiom. However, as these scores are not in a published form, the reader may have to substitute other scores that merit careful investigation.

Alternate Text Possibilities:

The Contemporary Arranger *(Don Sebesky)*

The Professional Arranger/Composer *(Rusell Garcia)*
The Garcia book is about thirty-five years old, but still a fine book for basic arranging techniques. Sebesky's book is a fine book for putting 'polish' on more-advanced writers. The books by Dick Grove and Gordon Delamont should also be investigated as possible texts.

Additional Teaching Suggestions

Some time will have to be spent with familiarizing the students with ranges, transpositions, and idiosyncracies of the many instruments for which they will be scoring and preparing parts. Special effects made possible by brass mutings should also be investigated, as well as woodwind doubling possibilities and the chairs to which those doublings should normally be assigned. Have them listen to some Gil Evans scores, with their many hybrid combinations (mixed mutings, high woodwinds with brass, etc.) and challenge them to identify those combinations. Have them listen, also, to some of Duke Ellington's recordings, for the same reason, and to identify which instrument(s) has (have) the lead and where that voice occurs within a stacked chord.

As various scoring possiblitities are taken up, in the text or from the instructor's notes, urge the students to keep a list of those techniques, so that they can refer to the list while they are scoring, to remind them of their many options.

When it is time to have their arrangements played by an ensemble, remind the students not to judge themselves too harshly if they're disappointed by what they hear. When you add the performance of a score to what you were hearing as you wrote it, there is often a discrepancy that is not necessarily the arranger's fault. This author has heard great arrangements being sight-read by an ensemble in which the resulting sound was deplorable. The student has to learn to distinguish between performance problems and compositional problems.

Advanced Improvisation

Text: ***Wayne Shorter play-along*** *(Aebersold, Vol. 33)*

Week 1	Distribution of syllabus and hand-outs (4 pertaining to In-Class Performances, plus "Interval Patterns"). Begin "Interval Patterns" (continuing until all have been done in class) and the playing of melodies in 12 keys (melodies selected by instructor).
Weeks 2-4	Demonstration of In-Class Performance by instructor, followed by discussion of problems to be solved in such a project. Continuance of Interval Patterns and various melodies in 12 keys. Study and performance of tunes using the Coltrane Matrix ("Giant Steps," "Countdown," etc.).
Weeks 5-6	Improvisation in 12 keys (Blues, "Stella by Starlight," "Ladybird," etc.). Ear training with improvisation (on tapes). Begin work on In-Class Performance tape.
Weeks 7-9	Study of "I Got Rhythm" progression, in 12 keys, at various tempos, and with common devices used on that progression. Begin tempo study (ca. 180-320).
Weeks 10-12	Perform tunes from Wayne Shorter play-along.
Weeks 13-14	(approx.) In-Class Performances by each member of class, plus 'post-mortem' discussion after each.
Week 15	Final examination (written).

Hand-outs/Supplements

Interval Studies.
Tempo Study (see following pages).
Instructions For In-Class Performances, Preparing A Tune For Performance, And In-Class Performance Evaluation (see following pages,

all pertaining to'in-class performances').
List of devices to be used with "I Got Rhythm" progression.
Copies of tunes used for study of Coltrane matrix.
Copies of tunes used for 12-key study (such as "Stella By Starlight", "Ladybird", and others).
Instructor will need some ear-training tapes for use in class.

Alternate Text Possibilities:

Any play-along which has a number of good, but difficult contemporary tunes, such as Aebersold's Volume 4 (Movin' On), Volume 9 (Woody Shaw), Volume 10 (David Baker), Volume 19 (Dave Liebman), or Volume 35 (Cedar Walton).

The Music Of Ron Miller would be very appropriate, if it was not already covered in the sophomore course, and the new Liebman-Beirach play-alongs *(Quest-Standards)* from Advance Music are fine for this purpose. Some instructors may want to put together a composite tape for Advanced Improvisation, similar to what this author does for the sophomore improvisation courses.

Although no text book was specified for this course, a good possibility for that purpose would be *Advanced Improvisation* (David Baker).

Additional Teaching Suggestions

As it was described in Chapter 2, the Advanced Improvisation should focus on topics which would have been too difficult for beginning improvisers, such as playing melodies and improvising in all keys, fast tempo study, improvising at sight on 'new tunes', learning to layer chord substitutions and special devices over blues and "I Got Rhythm" tunes, interval studies, working with the Coltrane matrix, playing over drones, more contemporary vehicles, and an emphasis on aesthetic values. The course also affords some time to quickly review some aspects of the sophomore course which were difficult enough to require considerable self-application during the ensuing year.

Since this course is possibly the last formal course the students will take in improvisation, the instructor needs to use it as an opportunity to fill gaps, eliminate weaknesses, re-check their theoretical understanding, set their attitudes toward improvisation for life, teach them how to troubleshoot their own problems provide them with a list of still more things to be accomplished *after* graduation (this author's list is entitled, "Where Do We Go From Here?").

Tempo Study

Ostensibly, this study is meant to facilitate the playing of especially fast tempos. However, it is intrinsically tied to several other facets of playing at any tempo. The player must learn to identify his/her problem precisely, if the problem is to be solved with any degree of efficiency. Some of the possible causes for experiencing difficulty with playing tempos are:

(1) a lack of instrumental technique, in terms of finger speed. Actually, this is relatively rare, as evidenced by the ability of most players to execute rapid trills, glissandi, and fall-offs with reasonable ease. It is, nonetheless, one possibility;
(2) difficulty with focusing enough attention on the pulse that is provided by the drummer and bassist, due (usually) to getting caught up in the intricacies of improvising;
(3) inappropriate jazz phrasing, such as over-articulating or having problems with playing swingy eighth-notes (i.e., playing dotted-eighth/sixteenths instead of something closer to a 12/8 feel). No one can actually tell you how to swing, though you might come close by using the 12/8 feel, accenting upbeats, and tongueing upbeats and slurring into downbeats. But even those applied interpretations will only simulate the real thing. Listening to players who are unanimously felt to swing especially hard is probablу the best way to discover the swing feel.

Even if the player experiences no difficulty with any of the foregoing, most players have a breaking point, with respect to good *pulse relation.* That is, although they have the technique, phrasing, and ability to listen to their musical surroundings (the latter possibly still part of the problem) after a certain point in the tempo spread, careful listening will reveal that the player is no longer *coinciding* with the provided pulse. This is more a problem of *controlled* technique, coordination, and a lack of experience playing the faster tempos. And this is more the problem being addressed in this study, though points 1-3 above must still be considered as contributing to the problem.

First the breaking point must be located, by selecting play-alongs that slowly climb the tempo scale, and listening carefully to detect the first signs of a breakdown in pulse relation. The following list is a possibility for such a play-along sequence, focusing on tunes which require very little effort, harmonically, so that the concentration may be placed on time-feel:

Tempo	*Title*	*Source*
190	In Case You Haven't Heard	JA-9
200	What Is This Thing Called Love	JA -15
224	Impressions (slower version)	JA-28
232	Tenor Madness	JA-8
240	F Blues with Bridge	JA-3
260	Mr. P.C.	JA-27
284	Nutville	JA-17
300	Impressions (fast version)	JA-28
320	Lover	RR-9

When the breaking point has been determined, note the tempo. Then, using a copy of a tempo legend (ask me for one), back up about 10-15 'notches' on the tempo (selecting any tune you wish at that tempo), and slowly work your way back up to, and hopefully past, the tempo that first gave you problems. Remember, if you have a tape player with variable speed, you can play the tune in a different key (and tempo), if the tune is not too difficult, giving you some tempo flexibility that can fill gaps where you don't own a listed play-along.

Each half-step change in pitch alters the tempo by about 14 notches.

Finally, the following list is provided as a helpful set of guidelines, while working with tempos:

(1) stay in 8th notes most of the time, using them as measuring units with the pulse;

(2) use more non-terminal patterns, diatonic substance, more chromaticism, 'machine licks', and in general, less angularity;

(3) listen more carefully to accompaniment than usual, thinking a little less about solo content;

(4) feel the tempo in 2, instead of 4, so as to minimize tension;

(5) plan (or look) ahead more, concentrate harder, and don't wilt or fall into too many short, choppy phrases;

(6) lengthen phrase units;

(7) *sing* some choruses before playing them, so you won't be distracted by the problems of playing the instrument;

(8) strive for an *emphatic* feeling of swing and phrasing, for building a sense of conviction and commitment;

(9) consider learning to play some drums or bass (it certainly worked for Mike Brecker, Randy Brecker, and Dave Liebman, among others!);

(10) in your practice (when not using play-alongs), increase dramatically the tempos of 'heads', patterns, scales, etc., perhaps using a metronome.

Instructions For In-Class Performances

In the second half of the term, each of you will be scheduled to give a mini-concert with play-along tapes, during a regulary-scheduled class meeting. Each performance will last approximately 30 minutes, so there will only be one performer on any given day. Informal critiqueing by the other members of the class will follow each performance. Students who are absent from any performance by a classmate will automatically receive a lower score on *his/her* performance. All material played must be memorized by the performer, including program order, melodies, changes, number of choruses on each tune, introductions, and ending. Each performance will be taped and graded by me.

Procedure

* Using one of the provided lists of play-along tunes, select one tune from each of the following vehicle-types:

standard
bebop
modal
blues
contemporary
ballad

* The ballad must be within the tempo range of 42-80 (100 is an absolute maximum).
* At least one tune must be at a tempo of 232 or above.
* Include one tune which is played in some other key than the original, by using a tunable tape player. It cannot be a blues or a modal tune.
* Except, possibly, the ballad and the modal tune, all tunes should have a melody chorus at the beginning and the end.
* Decide upon a program order, then produce your own play-along

concert tape, dubbing the tunes in the correct order, giving yourself a tuning track at the beginning (that is consistently maintained for all subsequent tracks, which won't have a tuning track), and the tune that you use in an un-standard key already re-tuned for the dubbing.

You will be graded on every aspect of the performance, including the tape, the quality of the selected tunes, memorization, interpretation, conception, timefeel, intensity, intonation, scale choices, presence of appropriate melodic pattern materials, program order, etc., and your presence at all in-class performances.

Much of what we work on in the first half of the term will help you with your graded performances of the second half, so work hard at everything we take up.

Start work on your performances as soon as possible! It will take time.

Preparing A Tune For Performance

(1) Acquire an accurate lead line/changes.
(2) Acquire the best 1-3 recorded versions of the tune.
(3) Listen many times to the recordings, with lead line/changes in hand.
(4) Sing with the recordings (head, solos, backgrounds, etc.).
(5) Check the accuracy of the lead sheet against the recording.
(6) Jot down any chord substitutions you hear being used on the recordings.
(7) Memorize the lead line and changes.
(8) Play the progression in several other keys (on piano as well).
(9) Transcribe the best solo on the recording, analyze it, and play and sing it.
(10) Practice (on your instrument) and sing head with recording (original recording).
(11) Practice and sing head with a play-along (buy or make play-along).
(12) Practice and sing transcribed solo with play-along.
(13) Examine sources for your own improvisation (head, transcribed solo, etc.).
(14) Practice scales, patterns, and licks with play-along.
(15) Practice intensification devices (volume, range, rhythm, harmonic intensity).
(16) Improvise many, many choruses with play-along.

In-Class Performance Evaluation

Advanced Improvisation
Music 4860 name:______________________

Memorization **Comments**

__ program order (0-3)

__ format (intros, endings, no.cho.) (0-4)

__ melodies (0-10)

Program Quality

__ quality/appropriateness of selections (0-5)

__ order of selections (0-3)

__ quality of tape-dubbing (0-3)

__ ballad tempo of 42-80 (✓ only)

__ bright tempo of 232+ (✓ only)

__ non-standard key (✓ only)

Standard - title:

__ melodic phrasing (0-2)

__ chord-scale accuracy (0-2)

__ key shifting (0-2)

__ presence of patterns (0-2)

__ time-feeling (0-2)

__ overall quality of improvisation (0-2)

Bebop - title:

__ melodic phrasing (0-2)

__ chord-scale accuracy (0-2)

__ key-shifting (0-2)

__ presence of patterns (0-2)

__ time-feeling (0-2)

__ overall quality of improvisation (0-2)

Modal - title:

__ melodic phrasing (0-1)

__ non-terminal patterns (0-1)

__ melodic development (0-2)

__ intensity-building (0-2)

__ pentatonics/fourths (0-2)

__ side-slipping/outside playing (0-2)

__ overall quality of improvisation (0-2)

Blues - title:

__ melodic phrasing (0-2)

__ story-telling/riffiness (0-2)

__ emotion/intensity (0-2)

__ time-feeling (0-2)

__ improvisational melodic conception (0-3)

Contemporary - title:

__ melodic phrasing (0-2)

__ chord-scale choices/accuracy (0-5)

__ overall quality of improvisation (0-5)

Ballad - title:

__ melodic phrasing (0-3)

__ chord-scale choices/accuracy (0-3)

__ rhythmic volatability (0-3)

__ improvisational lyricism (0-3)

______ **Score Total**

______ **Letter Grade**

Jazz Pedagogy

Text: ***The Teaching Of Jazz** (Coker)*
***The Jazz Ensemble Director's Manual** (Lawn)*

Week 1	Examination of motives for teaching jazz, and the job market and graduate assistantships in jazz education. Qualities of a good jazz educator. Hand-outs pertaining to lecture/demonstrations to be delivered by each member of class.
Weeks 2-4	Examination of jazz curricula at other institutions Rationale for the curriculum developed by Coker (at U.T., Miami, and other places). Each class member will design his/her own jazz curriculum, to be included in an extensive personal notebook for teaching jazz (to be turned in at end of semester for grade).
Weeks 5-8	Survey of texts, syllabi, audio-visual materials, and studio office materials needed for operating a collegiate jazz program. Student lecture/demonstrations will begin at about this time.
Weeks 9-13	Study of the needed techniques for rehearsing jazz ensembles, to include repertoire, programming, concert producing, conducting frames, rehearsal techniques, and practice-conducting with tapes, culminating in a 20-minute (approximate) graded conducting of a jazz ensemble.
Week 14	Turn in notebooks for grading. Jazz ensemble adjudication, using tape (in class).
Week 15	Return notebooks to students (for possible future reference). Return and discuss results of jazz ensemble adjudication.

Hand-outs/Supplements

Collection of announcements of position openings and available graduate assistantships in jazz at various universities, from the preceding year and the current year. These are not given to the students, but they are passed around in class, discussed, and made available upon request.

Collection of current publishers lists of jazz ensemble arrangements, alphabetized (by company), bound, and placed on reserve in library, along with demo tapes, records, and soundsheets.

Collection of brochures, curriculum information, and catalogs from other universities which offer jazz degree programs, placed on library reserve.

Copies of adjudication forms for jazz ensemble festivals, to be used by students in practice adjudication (in the likely event that they are someday asked to be one of the judges at a festival).

A tape for the practice adjudication, including several school levels (high school, small or 2-year college, university) and several levels of ability (poor-superior).

Poster-size diagrams of conducting frames, both squared and rounded versions, for all meters, to be used in class by instructor.

A tape of excerpts from various recorded jazz ensembles, with examples of all meters, mixed meters, and tempos, to be used in class for practice conducting.

Hand-outs pertaining to student lecture series, adjudication forms for same, and adjudication forms for practice conducting of live ensemble (see following pages for samples of all three forms).

Hand-out entitled, "Suggestions For Handling Jazz Ensembles" (on following pages)

Alternate Text Possibilities:

Jazz Pedagogy *(David Baker)*

***The Jazz Ensemble** (Robert Henry)*

The Henry book has gone out of print, but the instructor may be fortunate enough to locate a copy in a library. Like the Lawn text, Henry's book is a book on directing jazz ensembles, not a complete jazz pedagogy text. This author used to require both Lawn and Henry, as the two books complement each other.

Additional Teaching Suggestions

Although the jazz curriculum presented in this book does not show it, in at least two of the universities where this author has established jazz degreee programs, the Jazz Pedagogy course material was split into *two* courses, with the second course being called Jazz Directing. A glance at the syllabus will reveal that there really are two divisions to the course, the first being more comprehensive with regard to topics, the second restricted to learning to rehearse and conduct jazz ensembles. The reader may wish to adopt the two-course plan, if the number of credit hours permits a choice, as the nature of the two major segments of the pedagogy course shown here are really quite different.

A number of additional topics for pedagogy were mentioned in Chapter 2 in the preliminary discussion of the course. The reader may wish to refer to that list and consider using some of those optional subjects.

Lecture Series By Jazz Pedagogy Students

Each member of the Jazz Pedagogy class will give a one-hour lecture as part of the course requirements. The procedure will be as follows:

(1) Each class member will draw a topic 'out-of-a-hat' (I'll provide).

(2) Each student will carefully prepare his topic (all topics have a sufficiently narrow scope to permit good coverage in an hour), including lecture notes, records/tapes, playing demonstrations (some on piano, hopefully), and whatever audio-visual materials seem appropriate (posters, chalkboard, overhead transparencies, etc.).

(3) Each lecturer will be responsible for all aspects of set-up, such as placing of piano, table screen, etc., and seeing to it that the room is equipped with what you need. You may ask me questions about these things in advance, but on the date of the lecture you're on your own... so don't wait til the last minute to prepare.

(4) I will have posters made for each lecture, showing when, where, who, and what (topic), inviting anyone who wishes to come, so your audience will probably be musically-attuned, perhaps even attuned to jazz, as the posters will primarily be displayed in the music building. This permits you to cover your topic without trying to accomodate the level of musical understanding of your audience.

(5) All lecture/demonstrations should allow for at least 5 minutes of questions from the audience (including me) at the close of the meeting.

(6) All other members of the class are expected to be at each lecture/ demonstration (it would be to your advantage, anyway... could pick up some ideas for your presentation).

(7) The dates will be carefully selected at our meeting in which the topics are drawn.

(8) You are strongly advised to prepare well ahead of time, rehearse your lecture and demonstrations, and time your presentation as though it were an ongoing course with limited meeting time (50 minutes, really, rather than an hour). I will cut your presentation, after a maximum of one hour, if need be, as you need to get into the habit of staying within the allotted time.

(9) You will be graded on the quality of your presentation and I will be adjudicating as well, giving you a comment sheet afterwards.

Adjudication Form For Jazz Pedagogy Lecture/Demonstration

Student Lecturer: ______________________________

Presentation of Topic:

____ accuracy
____ clarity
____ completeness
____ organization

Audio-Visual Materials:

____ hand-outs
____ chalkboard
____ overhead or opaque projector
____ tapes, records

Demonstrations:

____ on major instrument
____ on piano
____ singing

Classroom Manner:

____ audibility
____ vitality
____ confidence

Clock-time:

____ started on time
____ 45 min. lecture
____ 5 min. question and answer period

General Comments:

grade ____________
adjudicator______________________

Adjudication Form For Jazz Directing

Name ______________________________ Date __________

Selection ______________________________________

	Specific Comments
Attentionality	
Tune Up	
Verbal Directions	
Count-Off	
Tempo	
Time-Feeling Image	
Balance/Dynamics	
Conception/Demonstration	
Conducting	
Cue-ing	
Cut-offs	
Individual Visiting	
Efficiency	
Total Average	

General Comments:

Adjudicator ______________________________

1 - excellent

2 - good

3 - adequate

4 - needs work

5 - relative failure

Suggestions for Handling Jazz Ensembles

I. Repertoire

A. Criteria for selecting music:
   (1) Purposes and goals of ensemble (i.e. educational, functional, etc.).
   (2) Stylistic/historical considerations.
   (3) Level of ability.
   (4) 'Training' materials (easier charts, training books, sight-reading material).
   (5) Performance material.
   (6) Musical quality and stylistic validity (in both training and performance).

B. Sources:
   (1) Published material.
   Many companies;
   a) get on their mailing list
   b) some include demo tapes, sound sheets, or LP's
   c) check NAJE Journals for evaluated, graded listings.
   (2) Colleagues and friends.
   Trade xeroxed original (unpublished) charts.
   (3) Professional 'hand-me-downs'.
   a) from cooperative bandleaders
   b) from guest artists
   (4) Products of arranging classes (student's charts).
   (5) Commissioned compositions/arrangements (rare, due to cost)
   (6) Charts written by yourself.
   Arranging class products, commissioned works, and self-written charts have the advantage of being customized to suit the abilities of ensemble.

II. Library System and Maintenance

A. To avoid unnecessary losses:
Don't place entire repertoire in individual folios (pass out charts as needed and call in charts that don't need to be in folios at the time)

B. Alphabetizing vs. numbering:
 (1) Alphabetizing works better for files, making for easier location.
 (2) Numbering works better if band plays dances, where it is easier to call up sets by numbers from folios.

C. Use lists or file card system for easier scanning of charts in filing cabinet.

D. Select an envelope for filing charts that provides information such as title, composer, arranger (helpful when making up printed programs), instrumentation, level of difficulty, style, tempo, solo designations, lead trumpet range, woodwind doubles, whether a score or conductor's guide is included, and whether there are any parts missing.

E. Take inventory at end of each year of all parts that were in folios, to check for missing or damaged parts.

F. Stamp parts and folios with school identification and address, in case of loss while on trip (concert tour, festival, etc.).

III. Rehearsal Techniques

A. Study score carefully, before going to rehearsal:
 (1) Listen to a reference recording, if available.
 (2) Know the ideal tempo and what part of chart helps to determine that tempo (certain sections will only sound well if the tempo is right).
 (3) Memorize sections, rehearsal letters/numbers, placement of solos, etc.
 (4) If both a complete score and a conductor's guide are available,

use the full score at the first rehearsal (for checking notes), and switch to the conductor's guide after that (to avoid handling excessive numbers of pages, to have a more concise reference, and to accomodate more eye contact with band.

B. Conducting techniques:
   (1) Learn conducting frames for all meters, but only conduct frames when it is needed.
   (2) Learn to alter frames to accomodate rhythmic figures where needed.
   (3) Learn to conduct in subdivisions of any meter.
   (4) Learn to cue entrances.
   (5) Learn a clear cut-off motion, perhaps two (one for stopping the band quickly in rehearsal to solve a problem, another for ending fermatas).
   (6) Stay in motion, even when not conducting frames, so that anytime the members happen to glance at you, your motions are always reflecting the mood and spirit of the music.
   (7) Try to avoid the podium approach, being ready to move around the rehearsal area as needed, focusing on sections and individuals, and whispering in the ears of individuals who need help (without stopping entire ensemble).

C. Attitudes upon entering rehearsal:
   (1) Be relaxed, but involved and full of expectations.
   (2) Imagine the perfect version of the chart, don't let their 'imperfect version' cause you to forget the perfect version, and don't settle for compromises or less than their best effort.
   (3) Be ready to trouble-shoot, patiently.
   (4) Listen carefully to the soloists, help them, and praise them.

D. Rehearsal activities:
   (1) Tune the band, sections, individuals.
   (2) Encourage pencil-markings (but never pens!).
   (3) Read new charts at the performance tempo at first, so they know

what the goal is, can more easily locate the problem spots, and won't be as likely to pull tempo down when you try to bring tempo back up after rehearsing trouble spots slowly (after the first reading, then rehearse at a slower tempo, to work out the problems).

(4) Rehearse chart in small fragments at first, to work out problems, then piece the fragments together.

(5) Be ready to sing phrases often to the band, for efficiency. Verbal descriptions and suggestions are good, but singing the phrase communicates articulation, accents, dynamics, feeling, etc. instantly.

(6) Don't forget to address problems of balance and dynamics!

(7) If you plan to play a certain chart in concert, start working on it early, then review it in each rehearsal, as it will continue to improve with time.

(8) After a strenuous, fragmented rehearsal of a chart, be sure to 'run it down from the top' without stopping, as it allays discouragement and illustrates to the band that even after a fragmented rehearsal to solve trouble spots it's difficult to remember and perform all details that were worked out when the events are continuous.

(9) Always try to begin and end the rehearsal on a positive note by having the band play something about which they can feel confident and successful.

IV. Programming

A. Decisions that must be made:

(1) How long shall the concert be?

(2) Will there be an intermission?

(3) Will there be breaks and/or talk between selections? How much? How long?

(4) Will there be more than one group performing?
(5) Will there be a guest artist?
(6) Will the director play?
(7) Who is the audience (4th graders, college-age, retirees, etc);

B. Program order and inclusion:
(1) Opener should be something which will set tone, warm-up band and audience, be a relatively assured performance success, and perhaps more traditional.
(2) Closer should be one of most exciting charts in program, though not neccessarily the most difficult or compositionally heavy.
(3) If there is an intermission, the selection just prior to the intermission shares, to some degree, the qualities needed in the concert closer, and the selection following the intermission is likely to be, to some degree a concert opener, though it is also a good place to schedule a small group.
(4) Weaker selections (such as a student chart, possibly) and low-key selections (ballads, bossa novas, modern but not spectacular charts, etc.) should be programmed in the middle of the first half of the concert (perhaps 2nd or 3rd).
(5) The concert climax chould be near the end, though perhaps next to last, rather than last, if it's very involved and heavy, compositionally.
(6) If an encore is needed, be ready for it, and play something that is exciting, but perhaps shorter and less-involved than the pieces just prior to that.

C. Other considerations:
(1) Assess the over-all inclusions, with respect to variety in mood, style, etc.
(2) Program the pieces in such a way as to promote contrasts between selections with regard to tempos, styles, moods, keys, players showcased, and endings.

(3) Program solos carefully,

a) put difficult solos in most capable hands,

b) give more solos to strongest players, but give some solos, perhaps shorter, easier ones to younger, budding players. Consider expanding (by editing) the solos of stronger players, as well as shortening the solos of weaker, though promising players.

V. Concert-Producing

A. Try to select dates that don't conflict with other events.
B. Consider acoustics of the place you have in mind.
C. Make up a detailed checklist, to include:
   (1) Printed programs.
   (2) Master-of-ceremonies script (memorized, hopefully).
   (3) Dress rehearsal/soundcheck in performance hall.
   (4) Physical equipment (possibly handled by a committee):
      a) stands
      b) chairs
      c) risers
      d) lighting (and someone to operate it)
      e) sound system (and someone very reliable to operate it)
      f) extensions cords
      g) bass stool
      h) recording equipment (and someone to operate it)
      i) music!
   (5) Band's attire.
   (6) Copy of program in each folio.
   (7) Band 'call' (not so early that they over-extend their warm-up, make unnecessary noise, create confusion, and get nervous).
   (8) Work on band's stage deportment.
   (9) Render pre-concert psychology:

Rehearsals are over, won't get a lot better than last rehearsal, relax, enjoy, listen to each other, etc.

VI . References

The Jazz Ensemble Director's Manual (Richard Lawn, C.L. Barnhouse Co., 1981)
The Jazz Ensemble (Robert Henry, Prentice-Hall, Inc., 1981)

Appendix

Each of us has varying degrees of different attributes for teaching, such as an organizational sense, orderliness, performing abilities, creative abilities, the ability to inspire students to do their best, scholarliness, innate musical taste, sociability, industry, aural abilities, philosophical and educational vision, conducting of ensembles, etc. We encounter teachers who can produce a great ensemble but can't remember to turn in grades at the end of a term or attend faculty meetings, and teachers who are scholarly and knowledgeable but relatively unloved by their colleagues and students. There are countless combinations and degrees of abilities and inabilities, substance and voids, and strengths and weaknesses. We should try to compensate and rectify these discrepancies, but some aspects of our weaknesses seem to haunt us all our lives. This appendix has several purposes. One is to round out and fill possible gaps in the body of the text. Another is to inspire through samples and examples. But the primary function is to help those who have difficulty with realizing a need, envisioning a solution, thinking of enough options, or simply have trouble organizing the needed paperwork of jazz teaching.

It is a potpourri of forms, attitudinal writings, lists, and articles, most of which are not course material, but extra little things which are a part of teaching or administrating a jazz program. I trust that some of it will prove interesting and/or useful to the reader, or at the very least, remind the reader that similar materials need to be conceptualized and prepared for the sake of his/her colleagues and students.

SMJ Entrance Examination/Questionaire

(1) ______________________________ (your name - please print)

(2) ______________________________ (your instrument)

(3) freshman ☐ transfer ☐ change of major ☐ (check one)

(4) What are your career goals, *specifically* (i.e. jazz performer, studio musician, teacher, songwriter, arranger, pop/rock performer, etc.)?

____

____

____

____

(5) Have you worked as a professional musician? ______________

How long? ____________________________________

(6) What tunes have you learned, if any, for which you've memorized both the melody and the chord progression?

____

____

____

(7) List some of your favorite musicians:

____

____

(8) What recordings by Miles Davis or John Coltrane do you own?

____

____

(9) Spell major scales in each of the following keys:

E ______________________________________

A-flat ___________________________________

(10) Complete the following blues progression, if you can:

F 7

| //// | | | | | |

| | | | | | ||

(11) Name the instruments played by the following jazz musicians:

Eddie Gomez ____________ Freddie Hubbard ________

Charles Parker ____________ Steve Gadd __________

McCoy Tyner ____________ J.J. Johnson __________

Wes Montgomery __________ Joe Henderson _________

Orientation For Studio Music And Jazz Majors

Welcome to the Studio Music and Jazz Program!
You have made a wise, practical choice for studying music, and if you apply yourself to that study, your chances of a successful, creative, and fulfilling career are excellent. You are very fortunate indeed that such a program has been made available to you (try to remember that!). The content of the SMJ curriculum has been painstakingly prepared for you to offer the best possible training in the jazz style. It is second to none anywhere in the world and has been widely imitated and adopted for its ideal content. Your jazz faculty is dedicated and experienced, and contrary to what you might find in jazz programs at other institutions, the members of your faculty are creative, successful performers in the professional world of music, and they are impervious to stagnation. You will also find that your non-jazz teachers of music are, by and large, equally dedicated to your learning process, many are fine performers and composers, and unbiased toward (even appreciative of) the jazz style.

As you expect a commitment from us, please understand that we expect a commitment from you as well. Knowing that it is a serious error to permit a jazz program to become too large and impersonal, the enrollment size of this program will never increase to more than 40 students. This insures your accessibility to the faculty and eliminates the possibility that you might just become a 'number'. It also promotes communication and coordination among the jazz faculty and insures that we can be sure that you live up to your commitment. What comprises this commitment?

(1) **Applied Lessons** - There are very few instances of 'one-on-one' situations in your education, but this is one of them. Appreciate the individualized nature of applied lessons... they are for you and you *only*. Don't miss lessons. If you're ill, call your instructor and let him know (*ahead* of the lesson time). Don't be late for lessons,

and practice, practice, practice!

(2) **Classes** - *Every* class is important, having been carefully prepared by the instructor, with new information, hand-outs, announcements, exercising of skills (*especially* in music), tests, opportunities to ask questions, etc. You deprive the other members of the class of your contributions when you're absent. *Nothing* takes precendence over being there, including gigs of the night before, lack of sleep for *any* reason, sexual attractions, or whatever. If you can't control your life's schedule, you have a very serious problem... one that will cost you a lot of gigs and opportunities for the rest of your life.

(3) **Orientation Meetings For Jazz Ensembles** - *Every* quarter, by the first day of registration, a list appears on the lobby bulletin board for jazz ensembles. It is a sign-up sheet, it will only remain posted until the first day of classes, then it is replaced by an announcement of the mass meeting in which you are split up into groups and rehearsal times are selected. It is *your* responsibility to get your name on the list and to attend the mass meeting. The fact that you have enrolled for the course is no help at that point, because the faculty won't be given class rolls until the 2nd or 3rd week, which is too late to start rehearsing groups. This system has been in effect for *many* years (*three* times per year), so don't profess ignorance. The mass meeting is also an opportunity to communicate with the SMJ majors in a rare meeting of everyone. This list you're reading was probably given to you at such a meeting. For starters, come to school *during* registration, *not after.*

(4) **Ensemble Rehearsals** - If every *class* is important, then multiply that importance serveral times more for ensemble rehearsals, as ensembles presume 100% attendance in order to function at all. When you're late, or miss a rehearsal, you let down *every member of the group*, not just the instructor and yourself.

(5) **Recital Attendance** - It is inconceivable that you would not

attend recitals, especially those given by your friends in the jazz program, but also those given by your music faculty, visiting artists, honors recitals, non-jazz music student friends, etc. *You* will one day give a couple of recitals, also. Watching others will help you to prepare and may insure that you won't be playing for an empty house. If nothing else, attend to support your friends.

(6) **Recital Participants (Assisting Personnel)**- If you accept an offer to play on someone's recital, and you should, make sure that it is an unwavering commitment. There will be rehearsals and a recital hearing as well as the recital itself. Don't let everyone down by accepting outside gigs at times when you agreed to rehearse or perform. It's good to accept gigs, but keep your priorities straight when dates conflict.

(7) **Jazz Pedagogy Lectures** - Each winter, during the Jazz Pedagogy course, members of the class are required to give public lecture/demonstrations on jazz, as part of their training. The course is required of *all* SMJ majors in the senior year. Because it is, for some, their first such presentation, no one can guarantee perfection (as it is with recitals), but you should attend for information, for preparation of yourself for doing it as a senior, and to support your friends.

If the foregoing list of commitments overwhelms you, then perhaps the jazz program, your development as a creative player, and your ensuing career is also too much for you. Perhaps you should look for something less challenging in which to major. This is a good program, it is joyously creative, and heavily-loaden with career opportunities. But anyone who tells you that it is *easy* is either a liar or ignorant of the facts.

A number of papers, forms, and lists have been prepared for SMJ majors to help you through the program. They are *extremely* important to you (not optional), so be sure you obtain a copy when you need it. Ask for it by number (for example, should you lose this form, it is SMJ-

6). All jazz faculty members have copies to distribute as needed.

SMJ-1 - SMJ brochure (this one and the next 2 are for new student inquiries)

SMJ-2 - SMJ curriculum

SMJ-3 - Entrance requirements for SMJ majors

SMJ-4 - Written exam/questionnaire for new SMJ majors (not available in advance)

SMJ-5 - Registration aids for SMJ majors (for self-advising. Everyone should have)

SMJ-6 - Orientation for SMJ majors (this form)

SMJ-7 - Proficiency procedures (get one now!)

SMJ-8 - 3-level tune list for proficiencies (get this one now, also from your applied teacher, as they differ for different instruments)

SMJ-9 - List of suggested books, methods, and play-alongs to purchase

SMJ -10 - Recital guidelines for SMJ majors (don't try to give a recital without acquiring a copy of this, as it is absolutely necessary)

Jazz Juries

At the end of each term all SMJ majors are required to take a jazz jury. The *fall quarter jury* will consist of preparing and memorizing a tune of your choice. 2nd, 3rd, and 4th year students are also required to improvise on the tune. The *winter quarter jury* will consist of melodic sight-reading. Pianists and guitarists will also be expected to sight-read changes, and bassists will be expected to play a walking line to the changes they're sight-reading. The *spring jury* will consist of improvising over a progression that is being sight-read.

Perpectives On Being An SMJ Major

Amidst countless distractions, it is difficult to retain one's perspective with regard to being a student in a university degree program. For starters, you are here to learn, so make a firm commitment to *all* of your courses. Be punctual, give each class (or rehearsal) your full attention, submit all assignments on time, study consistently, and let nothing deter you from the successful completion of each and every course. If you think the course is pointless, for your purposes, let us know how you feel about it and why, but bear in mind that people of your age frequently don't perceive the value of something until considerable time/experience has taken place. If your schedule seems awesome, organize your time so you can cope with it ... and stick with the schedule you devise for yourself. If you get 'burnt-out' with being a student and feel you must at least have a break in the action, try to anticipate your needs, so that you complete the term you are in at the time, in a graceful way. It will serve no purpose to simply 'flake' in the middle of a term - to the contrary, you may find that you have burned your bridges, foregoing the option to return at will. If you do decide to take a 'breather' from school, be sure that you really need and deserve it, and that you make good use of the time while you are away.

Respect your teachers. They're obviously not in their activity for money, fame, or even your gratitude. They're in it because they believe in education, creativity, and *you*! Whatever imperfections you perceive, or think you perceive, are of little significance, considering the batting average of the human race (which includes you as well). They're trying. Whenever you have doubts about others, try to imagine yourself in the same situation as theirs and *then* imagine what you would specifically do to improve the situation... then share that idea with your teacher. You might be surprised to learn how many of us are continually searching for better answers. Whatever you do, don't simply sulk or resort to unkind remarks... that's too easy. I have been a teacher in *many* universities, probably more than you'll even *see* in your lifetime, and believe me when I tell you that you are studying in one of the very best jazz programs in one of the very best music schools anywhere. It is understandable that you cannot perceive this, but I can. Don't be deceived by the low profile we are forced to keep. It's not a famous music school, just a great one.

Respect the cost of your education, regardless of whether it is paid for by you, your family, the school, or any combination of the foregoing. The monetary cost, even at an inexpensive school like this one (one of the reasons I came here), is one of the largest investments that will be made in your behalf for the remainder of your life. Don't blow it!

Finally, remember always that your future is already being shaped by your present actions. You may *think* of yourself as merely a student with all the attendant freedoms to be a child, mouth off, screw up, sleep late, experiment with lifestyles, have fun, etc., etc., but if that's what you think, you're deluding yourself. Your adult life is already under way, like it or not, so that your present behavior is already affecting your future, for better or for worse. Your effectiveness as a musician ***and your reliability as a person*** are *already* affecting whether or not you are recommended for playing gigs, graduate assistantships, composing/arranging assignments, and teaching positions. The game of life requires that we make accurate, honest assessments of people we recommend for *anything*. Otherwise we lose our credibility, people don't call on us anymore for recommendations, and countless opportunities are lost for others. ***Your future is now!***

APPENDIX

To My Jazz Piano Students

Whether we like it or not, others measure our level of musicianship primarily on the basis of our instrumental ability. I have known many teachers, composers, and musicologists who, though excellent at their craft, suffered a loss of respect because of a lack of the *ability* to play with a reasonable degree of proficiency or mastery on their instruments. *Some* of them do indeed play very well, despite their absorption in a relatively non-performing area of music, but many others do not. The point is, *no one* fares well in the eyes of others if their performing ability is weak, especially if their focus *is* performance.

A recent survey of the applied faculty at U.T. showed that they expected their students to practice *at least* as many hours daily as the number of credit hours taken. For example, a student taking applied lessons for three hours credit is expected to practice at least three hours a day. Many of the faculty also specified *seven* practice days weekly, rather than five, and some felt that a student working toward a *career* in performance needed even more hours of daily practice. We also know that legendary jazz figures like John Coltrane, Art Farmer, Sonny Stitt, etc., were known to practice anywhere from *five* to *eleven* hours daily ... and *they* were especially gifted from the outset!

Long hours of daily practice, on a consistent basis, are absolutely essential and most assuredly rewarding to the player. If you don't like to practice, or are incapable of organizing your time and energy toward consistent practice, then you should think twice about pursuing a career in music. And you should consider making time and space for someone who *is* seriously determined to make the effort. If, on the other hand, you *want* to succeed, and are willing to make the necessary commitment, then start *now* and let *nothing* stand in your way (especially yourself)!

Starting now, these are the ground rules for any jazz piano student who wishes to study with me:

(1) all three credit hour students will be expected to practice at least three hours per day;
(2) every lesson will be graded A-F;
(3) lessons missed without proper notification will be graded F and will not be re-scheduled;
(4) lessons that are re-scheduled will not receive a higher grade than a B;
(5) learning of assigned scales, patterns, transcribed solos, and bass lines will be considered equally important as tunes, improvisation, or recital preparation (none of the latter items are sufficient reason to ignore the former items) and you will be graded accordingly on the *completeness* of your preparation of *all* assigned items; and
(6) all tunes assigned are to be memorized (melody *and* changes) by the next lesson. You may even be asked to perform changes and improvisation in at least one other key during your lesson.

If any of the foregoing *seems* unreasonable or harsh to you (it isn't), then please understand that I have your best interests for success in mind and heart. Also know that if you learn to meet the above conditions, you will win my undying respect and support. But even more importantly, you will gain in ability and *self*-respect!

On Learning Music

By Howard M. Roberts

If you are like most people, you probably learned how to play a musical instrument in the public schools. If so, then be aware that you have probably been programmed to learn in an inefficient and largely unrewarding way. As a result, many hours of practice have been lost because you cannot remember what you learned. And, obviously, if you can't remember it, you can't use it. You have wasted a great deal of time learning that learning music is all work and no reward - it is time to learn a new way.

The problem of the old way is that it depends for its success upon rote learning and ineffective methods of memorization. By contrast, the new way is compatible with the way the nervous system processes information and enables you to make progress in a natural and satisfying way.

It is essential to bear in mind that the valuable years of learning, which passed when you were very young and the nervous system was still being formed, have already been given up to the old way. Habits have been formed which are, for the most part, bad habits. These are destructive to the learning process, and will not contribute to your growth or pleasure in the study of music. However, simply recognizing these habits for what they are is not enough to get rid of them. You may consciously understand the new way, but the unconscious is in the grip of the old way and will prevail unless you constantly remind yourself. Presence of mind throughout the entire learning experience is necessary if you want to break the spell of the old habits. The new way may seem a little artificial to you because it is so unlike your previous training, but have faith - you will see results soon!

Now, let's look at the features of the new way. We will take up in turn; Quality, Quantity, Motivation, Diagnosis, Two Kinds of Memory, Recall, Time Frames, Accuracy and Speed, and Overload.

Quality

With the old way of learning, you are fed a piece of information of dubious relevance or importance and expected to master it for some future good which you do not presently comprehend. Because the information is not perceived to be of use to you, it is not well enough imprinted for easy recall. Then, six months later, when you need it for a particular application, you have to go back and learn it all over again. This has taken twice the time for half the musical payoff. This does not mean that you won't encounter material from time to time whose immediate relevance is not clear to you. You will. Should you ignore it and go on to the next assignment? The answer is no. Once your eyes, ears and hands have touched a thing, there is a kind of 'deja vu' effect which makes it much easier to remember later when the need arises. For this reason you should go through the regimen and discipline of learning that piece of information, knowing full well that you may not fully retain it this time around. There is however, a more efficient way to learn. It is based on the often heard but little appreciated rule that states: a person learns what he wants to learn when he wants to learn it. This is of the utmost importance in the selection of material. You must know exactly ***what*** you are working on and exactly ***why*** you want it. You must see how it fits into your present body of musical knowledge and how and where you will use it once you master it. Therefore, whenever possible, work only with information which has a useful purpose now.

Quantity

Let's talk for a moment about dealing with large quantities of information.

When approaching a new piece of music with hundreds of notes that you are supposed to learn, are you going to learn all of those notes simultaneously? The answer is - not likely. Nevertheless, it is possible to make the simultaneous learning of many notes appear to happen, as it does with good studio sight reading, but this is an illusion. They are still learning one note at a time, only the process is so accelerated as to seem like magic.

The old Chinese proverb "A journey of a thousand miles begins with a single step", changes the nature of the problem of learning altogether. ***You have only to play the first note successfully and properly to inform your nervous system that you are capable of playing that first note well and that you have now played your instrument correctly.*** You have now proven to yourself that you are a successful learner. Now you need only to build on this base - step by step, and the performance of the rest of the piece is merely a question of quantity rather than quality. In other words, if a student skier can ski the first three feet correctly, he certainly can ski the next three feet correctly and the next and the next. With this recognition comes strengthened motivation. The next note is easier to learn and the process accelerates. Just remember; after learning that first note, ask yourself simply - what is the next step? The obvious answer is - the next note. In this way, you are never overwhelmed by dealing with hundreds of notes at once.

The next step is just to put the first two notes together and perform them in sequence. You've now doubled the amount of material you've mastered without increasing the difficulty. Next? The third note and the fourth note ... and now all four together...!

Motivation

We are all accustomed to think that motivation results from the input we receive from others, whether this is a gold star, a word of encouragement, or even a failing grade. This is part and parcel of the old way of learning, but the motivation received in this way is short-lived. The only lasting and reliable source of motivation is successful performance, and only you can insure this. The self is the real source of motivation.

When you turn to a lesson and sit down to devote fifty minutes of your time and concentration, you must be assured that at the end of the period you will put your instrument down and walk away with what you sat down to get. You must give up the habit of failing and replace it with the habit of success. You've got to walk away with the reward every time, or know exactly what went wrong. With the new way, failure to learn and grow is eliminated by design. You will never walk away with a blank because you are confused about what you are doing or because of poor study techniques. But how do you determine what to do if something does go wrong? This brings us to diagnosis.

Diagnosis

In your studies it is very important to be aware of the effects of environmental factors such as weather, light, and background noise.

If it is a hot, stifling day, and the oxygen count is low, your learning is going to be affected. Improper lighting can cause fatigue and eye strain. Be sure that your practice area is well-lit; if you are particularly sensitive to this problem you might solve it with full-spectrum lighting, etc. Next, be aware of distracting noises in the environment. We live in a world of 60-cycle hum. The electricity in all of our walls is humming away, producing a pitch somewhere between b-flat and b-natural. If there is an air conditioner or refrigerator nearby, the sound can influence everything you play. You can be severely out of tune with the refrigerator and easily mis-diagnose the problem as a fault of a tin ear or lack of talent.

All of this points to a larger concern - the problem of properly diagnosing and identifying the obstacle to successful and rewarding learning. You might think, for instance, "No matter how hard I try, I cannot play fast enough - there must be something wrong with my hands." The problem may actually be only the poor synchronization of two excellent hands. A possible solution is to play in the bathroom, where it is extremely quiet and resonant, and where one can hear the most minute detail coming out of the instrument. This may serve to eliminate quickly the flam-effect between the right and left hand.

Finally, relaxation is an important factor. Being relaxed affects your blood-flow and your muscle tone. Proper posture is equally important. Get up from your chair, get the instrument out of your hands, and stretch frequently. If the task starts to seem overwhelming - lie down flat on the floor and breathe deeply for a few moments. Imagine yourself playing the passage perfectly. Be kind and considerate to yourself - after all you are learning to play music for the joy of it. Keep yourself relaxed and comfortable at all times, and your learning will be many times more effective.

Two Kinds Of Memory

There are two kinds of memory involved in the learning process. *Motor memory* is the training of the physical or motor skills (where to put your fingers, etc.,) and this requires that you train by repetition. If you are training motor skills, you can practice for many long hours without doing any harm. The more of this kind of repetition the better. In fact, much of this kind of learning can be accomplished unconsciously. A person can achieve wonders while mindlessly staring at the television, playing or noodling for hours, even with the sound on.

Data memory - the memorizing of conceptual data, such as scale construction, fingering patterns, licks, harmony, etc., you must work within very short time frames, making sure you do not exceed your attention span. Bear in mind that your attention span will vary from day to day, and may be as short as five, ten or fifteen minutes at any one sitting. The signal that you have come to the end of your natural attention span, may be anything from staring at the wall, to thinking about your vacation, to playing that little ol' blues lick you have known since you were seven. In this case, your unconscious mind is telling you, you have had enough for now. This is perfectly natural. So take a short break. It's no big deal. You'll recover quickly and you can continue on effectively.

Remember, then, that there are two completely different aspects to gaining musical control of the instrument: First, learning by mental rehearsal and visualization and recalling it from memory, and second (though no less important), motor skill training through repetition. Don't fall into the trap of confusing the two different types of learning and spending hours working without concentration trying to acquire conceptual data. And, conversely, don't be fooled into thinking that there is a short cut to acquiring motor skills.

Recall

Studies have shown that the mind is like a camera. Once it gets a clear impression of the material, the picture is snapped into focus. You have it. It can now be recalled and replicated in order to train the motor system. Memory should not depend on repetition. Rather, the rote learning we are taught in school is actually destructive to the learning process. What you should be doing is looking at the material once to get a very clear, focused picture; then, mentally rehearsing it without actually using the instrument. On the rote-memory system, you are taught to repeat the learning process over and over. This is where you start to forget. The picture blurs, and you do not learn how to remember.

Reinforce this new way of learning by staying away from the printed page as much as possible. Make the snapping of the image only once a matter of habit. Practice recalling the sounds and visualizing the fingerings that match those sounds. Do this while waiting for the bus or having lunch. In time this will become a second nature, and you will become a perpetual learner, able to learn as much away from the instrument as you can with it in your hands.

Time Frames

You may ask "How long should I work on new material at any one time?" The answer is, you should work on new material in the beginning in very short time-frames. A few minutes of concentrated, thoughtful study can make a solid impression and can prove far more beneficial than hours of unfocused drudgery.

In the beginning stages you will need to assign yourself breaks 'by the clock' until you become sensitive to your own physical and mental signals. So get yourself a kitchen timer and time each section of your practice.

At first, when your timer goes off signifying that your time is up, obey the discipline of the signal. Do not break it and go beyond your assigned time-limit! Then as you become more accustomed to managing your own time, you will become more and more sensitive to your own limits, and will be able to sense when you have gone too far and need to rest. Remember that, while on the old method it is all right to practice until you drop, the new method requires you to re-train yourself for a whole new kind of learning experience.

Accuracy And Speed

It is natural for any student of instrumental music to want to play fast right away. This is a perfectly legitimate desire. It is crucial to remember, however, that speed is a by-product of accuracy. If you are not accurate, your speed will simply not develop. If you try to play too fast too quickly you will simply reinforce the bad habit of sloppy playing.

The first mistake should serve as a signal, informing you not to do it again. That little mistake might not seem like much to the casual listener, but to you, engaged in the training of your motor system, that one mistake is far too costly to let slip by uncorrected. If you do let it go by, your nervous system will begin to view that level of performance as acceptable, and the mistake will become more and more difficult to overcome. So a rule to bear in mind is: Do not make the same mistake more than once. Multiple mistakes of the same type are very dangerous. Once you make a mistake - stop, go back and play it again more slowly - play only at a tempo which you can play without a mistake - then speed will come, naturally.

The Overload Problem

Now you might ask "All right, now I've broken the material down into very small sections, and I'm going to work on them slowly. But how many of these small sections can I keep in the air at the same time?" Here, you have to answer your own question. The process of assembling small bits of material is like a juggling act. If you're attempting to handle four small sections and at that moment you are only capable of handling three, adding the fourth can make you fumble the other three. So, if you feel a sense of overload, back off and concentrate on parts 1, 2, and 3. It's far better to leave your practice session with three bars of successfully accomplished study than to walk away with fifty bars of material you don't quite remember and can't quite execute. If you do subject yourself to overload, you will exhibit some discouraging symptoms. The most obvious symptom is not getting around to practicing - you just don't feel like doing it, even though you can't explain why.

You might wonder "After I become confident of my own ability to recognize things like loss of attention span and overload, should I still keep working within the time-frames imposed?" The answer to this question is that the management of time must always be kept in consideration; the chances are that it will never become completely natural to you, because your previous training is likely to be deeply ingrained. The chances are that you'll have to remind yourself constantly that you are in the business of adopting new methods for more efficient learning.

APPENDIX

Afterword

To become a well-rounded jazz musician will take time and patience. I don't recall anyone who has accomplished such a goal in less than two or three years, and I would guess that the norm is more like five years-or longer. When you stop to think that the average course in jazz at some institution of higher learning lasts four months, perhaps eight months for a two-semester course, it becomes obvious that we are exposed, intellectually, to many theoretical materials which cannot be fully assimilated at the time of presentation. Months and years will pass, perhaps, before such theoretical ideas are ready to be heard and played to satisfaction. Similarly, this book can be read in a relatively short time, yet it may be years before each of the ideas contained has been learned to the point that its usefulness is fully realized. For those who have difficulty organizing their practice habits, the time lag between presentation and fruition can be especially frustrating. To them I would like to offer some advice. Very few people use their time to maximum efficiency. Minutes and hours of time pass unnoticed by most of us every day. Learn to use those minutes and hours, rather than wait for a longer, 'more reasonable' time later. If there isn't time to do *everything*, then do *something*. It is better to concentrate on a smaller number of items, anyway, than to attempt everything in one session. If you laid five bricks a day, at the end of the year you'd have a 10` x 10` practice room. If you copied one part from a score each day (taking about twenty minutes), by the end of a year you'd have copied twenty-four arrangements for a fifteen-piece band. If you drive to school or work, put a tape player in your auto. If the trip is only twenty minutes each way, and you stay at home on evenings and weekends, you can still listen to about 165 hours of music (or 230 LPs) in a year. An average pattern for improvisation can be learned in about half an hour. If you practice a new pattern each day, in a year's time you'd have 365 patterns-more than the number (324) found in *Patterns for Jazz.* By following all these suggestions, at the end of the year you'd have a brick practice room, twenty-four arrangements copied (which also can bring in $250-$500), listened to 230 LPs, and gained 365 patterns! The foregoing illustrations may not coincide with your goals or the time span in which you hope to accomplish your goals, but whatever your goals and time availability, it should be obvious to you that without forsaking many, if any, of your present activities, you can become what you wish to be.

The Ear Can Be Cultivated

Many believe that people are either born with a 'musical ear' or not; and if not, there is little that can be done about it. This is not true and can be disproven in a number of ways. Achievement levels in the dictation that we usually find in a music theory course will show that while the level of difficulty increases, the grade curve remains about the same. Jazz musicians are usually at the top of the curve, too, because they have learned to use their ears in a more complete way than other types of musicians. Repetitious disciplines can train just about anyone to develop a musical ear.

The Memory Retains Everything That Has Ever Been Heard

It may take practice to learn to tap such a vast memory source, but it's all there. Most of us can hear music in our minds that is not, for the moment, being played or reproduced in an outside source. Whole selections can be heard in the mind this way, indeed, even whole LPs with their sequence of selections and keys can be 'played' in the mind. Often, we are not consciously aware that we are capable of this kind of memory-tapping. Each of us has had moments when we were unable to recall someone's name, for example, and said to ourselves,

"I'll think of it," or "It will come to me later." Sure enough, after a delay of anywhere from a few seconds to a few weeks, the elusive name drops into our consciousness, though we have not been thinking about it since the moment when we were first unable to recall it. At times such as these, the subconscious mind relays the information to the conscious mind. Had we made a negative suggestion to ourselves at the time of the memory lapse, like "I'll never think of it" or "Gone forever," we might have hindered the effort of the subconscious to look it up for us.

It is equally fascinating that *we are able to remember even the portions that are not understandable to us*, such as the types of chords that are being used, complicated solos, and massively orchestrated scores. We remember the sound, whether we understand it or not. Furthermore, we can learn to use our musical memory like a tape recorder, putting it in rewind or fast forward position.

The Ear Continues To Function In Sleep

Most people are aware that courses have been published on records that are meant to be played and absorbed in sleep, although little has been done with music in this manner. But we can even work on music in our dreams. Once, when I was slowly transcribing a choice piano solo by Clare Fischer, I had a dream in which I found myself sitting at a keyboard. I arrived at a place in the solo where I had not, in my waking life, been able to find the precise chord voicings he used. In the dream I continued right through the troublesome passage. I became excited about the discovery and awakened. I went to the piano to check what I had played in the dream and to my astonishment the passage was now correct.

A Precise Pitch Can Be Memorized

I first became aware of this fact while studying music theory in a class that was conducted by Dr. Roy T. Will. Dr. Will was a very well-organized sort of person who required that each student purchase an A-440 tuning fork and carry it with him at all times, listening to it as often as possible. At various points in his lecture, he would turn quickly to the class and ask us to sing A-440. At first our collective guess wasn't very impressive, but in a short while nearly everyone could remember and sing the pitch on call.

Any pitch can be raised or lowered slightly without becoming another note altogether. This is why musicians will tune up before playing - not to find the approximate pitch but the *precise* pitch (intonation).

I have often seen musicians who, taking their instrument from the case and without hearing another instrument, instinctively adjusted a tuning slide or mouthpiece after a few trial notes, sensing that they were flat or sharp in relation to some universal, more stable pitch. I also remember one instance in which a watch repairman challenged me to determine, without referring to an instrument or tuning device, the pitch of a watch that operated on a tuning fork principle. I was confused by the pitch, because it seemed to be *between* two semitones, so I answered that it was a pitch between two particular notes. The answer was correct.

By Association, The Ear Can Memorize Infinitesimal Differences In Tone Quality Between One Note And Another, Each Related To A Corresponding Pitch

Although quality-pitch correlation can be developed on virtually all instruments (Chet Baker, for example, used it with trumpet), the saxophone is a good example. Written 'c#' on the third space (treble clef) is played on a saxophone by raising all fingers, which causes air to escape through the tone holes long before the sound reaches the bell of the instrument. The resulting quality is thin and nasal, compared to other notes. Yet when the saxophonist moves from that 'c#' to a note that is only a semitone higher (d), he replaces nearly all the fingers to cover the holes in order to create that pitch. The resultant quality is hard and full, and *very* different from the 'c#'. Even the non-saxophonist notices the difference quickly. This means then that if I promise to play only one of those two pitches on a saxophone, *everyone* will know which is which, because of the *quality*. It follows that all notes, because they are fingered differently, have slightly varying qualities which, with careful observation, can be used to determine *all* pitches. On brass instruments, notes have differing qualities because the brass tubing is longer or shorter, depending upon which valves or slide positions are used. Stringed instruments have various material compositions (metal, gut, wound, etc.) that affect the quality, and open strings are recognizable. Once the ears are trained to hear the quality differences and associate those qualities with particular pitches and/or fingerings the player can begin to understand *spontaneously* what pitches he is hearing, either on a record or in his own mind. At that stage of development, he can also begin pre-hearing improvisations (practicing) without the instrument in hand, even creating new phrases, but always sure of the fingering and pitch. If he hears a different instrument than the one he plays - one on which he has developed quality-pitch association - he needs only to imagine each pitch being reproduced on his own instrument, and the ear and memory will come up with the corresponding quality for the pitch, as well as the fingering.

The Ear Can Hear Quality-Pitch Association On Additional Instruments

Learning quality-pitch association on one instrument does not mean that the student will not be able to develop the same ability on a related or unrelated instrument, or on an instrument of different pitch and/or range. Why do you suppose that, say, an E♭ alto saxophonist who tries to play B♭ tenor saxophone for the first time in improvisation often finds himself a fourth or a fifth interval away from what he thought he was about to play? Obviously, his pitch sense on alto was well ingrained, yet in a short while the problem abates, because he begins to hear tenor pitch. His alto pitch need not be disturbed in the slightest by taking on a new set of pitches to be related to quality. I have studied a number of instruments of different families and different pitches and I have yet to study one for very long before the quality-pitch association begins to work. I believe this is true for all players, whether they are conscious of it or not.

The Ear's Memorization Of Quality Is So Exact That Fingering Can Be Determined Even When Pitch Is Faulty

A friend of mine once brought a Duke Ellington record to my home to hear a Ben Webster solo I'd never heard. Since it was a tenor saxophone solo, I wasted no time applying the quality-pitch association to what I was hearing. At first I was somewhat flabbergasted at his technical fluency in the key I was hearing. But then I realized that the qualities produced by the various fingerings were *not* matching the correct pitch. Because the fingering does not change, I presumed the pitch to be incorrect. Sure enough, we discovered that the record was playing a semitone higher than it was recorded, changing the pitch but not the quality.

The Ear Can Be Trained To Quickly Recognize Any Musical Device That Is Widely Used And Heard Often

If I play a major triad or a major scale, for example, for a group of students, nearly everyone will recognize the device by ear without having to re-hear and study it for several minutes. It is an example of quick recognition. The same can apply to many other devices, as long as an effort is made. Such a list would include intervals, chords, scales, inversions of chords, progressions, key shifts, chord spacing or voicings, patterns, familiar motifs, chord function, note-of-chord function, melody-to-key relationships, diatonicism, and chromaticsm. It is the mark of a fine and well-trained musician to be able to quickly identify and use all such devices. Perhaps it is this ability that distinguishes the best from the merely good jazz artist.

The Ear Can Be Trained To Pre-Hear Phrases, Counterpoint, And Harmonies That Have Not Yet Been Played Or Written

Composers will often use this ability to 'audition' music in the mind before it is committed to paper. The effect is complete, and without needing to go to, say, a piano, he knows what the phrase will sound like. He can even project the sounds of the instrumentation used in his orchestration.

In this chapter we have been discussing, basically, the understanding of jazz style that is necessary to reproduce and create this kind of music. Learning to transcribe the music of recorded artists is vital in developing this understanding. So is developing a musical ear by constant training. Perhaps it would be safe to say that any really good musician - particularly jazz musician - is made, not born.

APPENDIX

Pretty: A Musical Definition Of The Word

People are generally in accord, surprisingly so, about what specific pieces of music could be called 'pretty'. There will be a few disagreements, to be sure, owing to the wide range of musical styles available and allowing for differences in listening habits, but not as many as might be encountered if we try to agree on what is *good* music. In other words, whatever musical ingredients are present when we sense a piece of music to be *pretty* must be somewhat universal in their potency, transgressing a lot of stylistic boundaries in the process. It should be obvious, too, that it wouldn't matter whether the music were to be a written piece of music or an improvised one. But what are these seemingly universal ingredients that spell 'pretty' in music? In general, those musical traits which tug at the heart and are *dramatic*, even gently so, are usually a part of what we sense as being pretty, and the word 'dramatic' is easier to understand, in musical terms, though not everything that is dramatic is necessarily pretty. But most everything that is pretty *is* dramatic. Below is a list of dramatic musical ingredients often present in music we think of as 'pretty'.

(1) **Tempo** and **Tempo Feel** - The two most dramatic tempos are very fast and very slow, all points in between being less dramatic *as a tempo* (though *other* musical aspects than tempo *could* cause drama at any tempo), and the very slow tempo having a much better chance of influencing a pretty result than a very fast tempo. Perhaps the very slow tempo relates to heartbeats better or maybe we are poignantly reminded of death and the slow funeral march, but at the very least, we can be sure that the ear has *more time* - to hear, to create, to embellish, to phrase, etc., and that alone could create a more dramatic or prettier feeling. Muzak clearly illustrates the effect of increasing a tempo distastefully to the point of becoming ridiculous (and not pretty) and mechanistic. In jazz, an improvising soloist *or* his accompaniment must guard the slow

tempo feeling or suffer a similar fate as Muzak .... sounding inappropriate, ridiculous, mechanistic, and not pretty.

(2) **Key**- Though a difficult point to prove, most sensitive musicians agree that certain keys are intensely dark, or brilliant. Songwriters seem to know this, too, hence Thelonious Monk placed "Round Midnight" in the dark key of E♭ minor, and Billy Strayhorn placed "Lush Life" in D♭ major, also dark and heavy. Singers often select very bright keys, like E major, though they could have (in terms of their range) selected a 'vanilla' key, like F major.

(3) **Mode** - Although many pretty tunes have been written in the major mode, there seems to be a universal preference for minor keys when trying to touch the heart of the listener. Even the pretty major tunes will often make a foray into a minor key somewhere in the tune, to heighten the dramatic aspect. In free-form improvisations, though no key or mode is stated, in most cases, there is a very strong tug toward lapsing into a minor key within a short time.

(4) **Modulations** - Most beautiful tunes rely on modulation sequences for dramatic effect. Modulations seem to symbolize a change of heart or a chance to begin anew. Modulations sometimes happen in sequences, such as the chromatically descending keys of Michele LeGrand's "Summer Knows" or George Gershwin's "Bess, Oh Where Is My Bess?", or a modulation sequence in which the keys descend by whole-step, like "Laura", "Little Boat", or "A Man And A Woman". Many tunes include a dramatic modulation at the B section (bridge), like Ellington's "Warm Valley" (B♭ major to E major) or "In A Sentimental Mood" (F major to D♭ major), or Strayhorn's "Chelsea Bridge" (A♭ major to E major). Countless show tunes have used a modulation up a major third for their bridge. Appendix D of *Improvising Jazz* (Coker) shows a multitude of modulation patterns on specific tunes. Even a simple modulation up a fourth can be a dramatic climax,

sometimes, especially if the new tonic (IV) becomes a minor seventh chord (after being a major seventh), so that it begins its fall back to the original key, as in the last 8-bar section of Matt Dennis' "Meaning Of The Blues". While it is true that an improviser can't do much about the modulation sequences that are already built into a tune (or not), he *can select* tunes which include dramatic modulations, which help to make for a more inspiring, dramatic improvisation (the same holds true for many of the points in this list).

(5) **Chord Extensions** - A dramatic phrase is often highlighted by 'leaning' on a note that is a note of the scale, but not a note of the basic chord (1, 3, 5, 7), in particular 9ths, 11ths, and 13ths. Consider all the 4 - 3 and 9 - 8 suspensions and appoggiaturas of J.S. Bach (and many others). In those days, such notes needed to resolve to a simpler chord tone, but in the present, those notes can, and should be, sustained for dramatic effect. Coltrane's "Naima" and Horace Silver's "Nica's Dream" consistently sustain 9ths and 13ths, for example, in their melodies. Improvisers have to look for these possibilities. Conversely, improvisers have to be careful about the use of simple notes, like roots, especially after a colorful chord/scale just prior to that point, as the dramatic-emotional bottom may fall out. Chord *alterations* (i.e., +9, ♭9, and +5) can also be dramatic.

(6) **Surprise Chords** - A chord that was not expected can become a dramatic device, as in chord substitutions, ending chords, and chords which are in the original version, but which are nonetheless a surprise.

(7) **Angluarity** - Both given and improvised melodies often are pretty because they leap (especially upward) by a wide interval such as 6ths, 7ths, octaves, or 9ths (i.e. Ellington's "I Got It Bad" which leaps a major 9th interval between the 2nd and 3rd notes of the melody, or LeGrand's "Summer Knows", which leaps by major

7th intervals several times during the bridge, or Coltrane's "Naima", which leaps down a minor 7th interval between the 3rd and 4th notes of the melody).

(8) **Embellishments** - Especially effective when they pull non-chord and non-scale (chromatic) notes into play, or delay a melodic or harmonic resolution.

(9) **Cesh** (**C**ontrapuntal **E**laboration of **S**tatic **H**armony) - very poignant and dramatic, both when built into tune (countless examples exist) and when improvised.

(10) **Chord-Types** - The most dramatic chord-types are dominant sevenths with augmented ninths and thirtenths, dominant sevenths with augmented fifths and augmented ninths, dominant sevenths with suspended fourths, diminished sevenths, half-diminished sevenths, and minor seventh chords with the seventh in the bass. Major seventh chords with an augmented fourth or an augmented fifth can also be very dramatic.

(11) **Pedal Point** - Used effectively in all styles of music, as in the ending of Stravinsky's "Firebird Suite", Joni Mitchell's "Cold Blue Steel", Coltrane's "Naima", and Joe Zawinul's "Midnight Mood", to mention just a few. A pedal bass simultaneously anchors the key and suggests that something important is about to happen. If the pedal is in a repeating rhythm, it oftens suggests a beating heart.

(12) **Range Climax** - Both good tunes and good improvised solos will make judicious, sensitive swells to the upper range. A good tune will often hold its highest pitch in abeyance until near the end, where it can help create an effective climax, as in J.J. Johnson's "Lament" or Matt Dennis' "Meaning of the Blues".

(13) **Phrasing** - Phrasing devices, such as bends, glissandi, vibrato, etc., especially those which imitate the human voice, are very dramatic and suggestive of speech-like storytelling.

(14) **Dynamics** - Like range climax, but more flexible, changes in

dynamic level suggest the rises and falls of moods, doing much to humanize the manner of expression.

The above list is meant to enhance, extend, and explore various means of creative, expressive, pretty feelings in music. The list was musically specific because 'pretty' is too vague a term to use when asking a young improviser to express beautiful music. Yet it must be said that any and all of the above means can do no more than put us in the ballpark ... for if we are to express beauty and love in music, we must also be sincere and our hearts must be attuned to that form of expression.

Harmonization And Reharmonization Techniques
Jazz Composition

(1) Combine II-7 chords with V7 chords (or any other 7 chords), when needed:

becomes:

D7	G7 || A-7 D7	D-7 G7
/ / / /	/ / / / || / / / /	/ / / /

(2) Substitute V7 sus4 chords for II-7 V7 progressions:

becomes: ... *or:*

D-7	G7 || G7sus4	% || G7sus4	G7sus4 G7
/ / / /	/ / / / || / / / /	/ / / / || / / / /	/ / / /

(3) When heading toward a temporary minor key within a major tune, add in IIø and V7alt. preceding temporary minor key:

becomes:

CΔ	(E7) %	A- || CΔ	Bø E7+5+9	A-
/ / / /		/ / / / || / / / /	/ / / /	/ / / /

(4) When heading toward a temporary *major* key within a *minor* tune, add in II-7 and V7 preceding temporary major key:

becomes:

C-	%	A♭Δ || C-	B♭-7 E♭7	A♭Δ
/ / / /		/ / / / || / / / /	/ / / /	/ / / /

(5) Precede IVΔ (in major tune) and IV- (in minor tune) with its own II and V:

becomes:

CΔ	%	FΔ || CΔ	G-7 C7	F
/ / / /		/ / / / || / / / /	/ / / /	/ / / /

or: ... *becomes:*

C-	%	F- || C-	Gø C7+5+9	F-
/ / / /		/ / / / || / / / /	/ / / /	/ / / /

(6) Try altering some unaltered dominant chords, especially V7 and VI7.

(7) Try adding and/or altering notes of simpler chords:

Δ+4 instead of Δ 7+4 instead of 7

Δ+5 instead of Δ ø9 instead of ø

-Δ instead of -7

(8) Add IVΔ chords in second half of duration of I chords:

```
                              becomes:
CΔ                            CΔ          FΔ
|/ / / / |       ./.         ||/ / / /   |/ / / /   |
```

(9) Look for opportunities to split duration of a chord with a chord that is a semi-tone higher:

```
                              becomes:
G7                            A♭7+4       G7
|/ / / / |       ./.         ||/ / / /   |/ / / /   |

or:          becomes:
CΔ           D♭Δ7+4 CΔ
|/ / / / ||/ / / / |
```

(10) Look for opportunities to create *chromatic* II-Vs in place of cycles (or any kind of symmetry):

```
E7           A7           D7           G7
|/ / / / |/ / / / |/ / / / |/ / / / |

becomes:
B-7 E7       B♭-7 E♭7     A-7  D7      A♭-7 D♭7
|/ / / / |/ / / / |/ / / / |/ / / / |
```

(11) Look for opportunities to substitute or add tri-tone substitutions:

```
                                        becomes:
D-7          G7           CΔ            A♭-7         D♭7          CΔ
|/ / / / |/ / / / |/ / / / ||/ / / / |/ / / / |/ / / / |

                                        or:
                                        D-7  G7      A♭-7  D♭7    CΔ
                                       ||/ / / / |/ / / / |/ / / / |
```

(12) Try using substitutes for I chords, as a surprise, such as III-7, ♭IIΔ, or ♭VIΔ.

(13) When going from I to IV, try putting a ♭V7 +4 between them:

becomes:

CΔ FΔ || CΔ G♭7+4 FΔ

| / / / / | / / / / || / / / / | / / / / |

(14) Try using CESH in place of some long duration minor chords or II-V progressions.

(15) On -7 chords, try moving bass note down to seventh in second half of chord's duration, especially if next chord is VI-7 (or ø) or a ♭VI chord:

becomes:

C- Aø || C- C-/B♭ Aø

| / / / / | / / / / || / / / / | / / / / |

(16) Try sustaining one pedal note against a sequence of chords:

becomes:

GΔ A♭Δ A-7 || GΔ /D A♭Δ /D A-7/D

| / / / / | / / / / | / / / / || / / / / | / / / / | / / / / |

(17) When harmonizing a given or already-written melody, consider letting longer notes (or repeated notes) function as 9, 11, +4, 13, ♭9, #9, etc., instead of root, 3, or 5.

(18) Try using Δ+5 in place of simple Δ sometimes (when melody is not on 5th, of course).

APPENDIX

Chord Substitutions

Jazz Composition

Chord substitutions are most commonly selected on the basis of common tones (between the given chord and its substitute chord) or common function. There are other means, of course, most notably the use of a substitute chord which simply accomodates or contains the given melody note. But since such melody notes cannot be anticipated in an *improvised* melody, the former means (common tones/common function) is bound to result in a more appropriate selection of substitute chords.

The lydian augmented scale (and its modes, such as ascending melodic minor, diminished-whole tone, locrian #2, lydian dominant, etc.) is a remarkably flexible scale, accomodating *five* types of chords: - Δ7 , ø, Δ7 (+5), 7(+4), and the altered dominant chord (+5, +9 or ♭9). These are by no means *all* chord-types that are possible, but they do represent many commonly-encountered chord-types. Furthermore, those chords which are accomodated by the major scale or one of its modes (dorian, lydian, etc.) are easy to deal with, and in the case of chords which utilize the diminished scale or whole-tone scale, like the 7 (♭9) (13) and the 7 (+5) (9) respectively, the choices are simple, because the scales are symmetrical (a C7 with a ♭9 and 13, for example, can be substituted for by a chord of the same type on E♭, F#, or A; similarly a C7 with a +5 and a 9 can be substituted for by chords of the same type on D, E, F#, G#, or B♭). The following chart, then, will focus on the chord-types accomodated by the lydian-augmented scale. To use the chart, simply locate the given chord root and type on the chart and select any of the other four chords shown on the same horizontal line. The 'unused chord root' columns are to aid the user in structuring slash chords with any of the five chordtypes shown on any horizontal line.

	-Δ	7 +4	9 7 +5	ø	Δ+5	**unused chord roots**	
E♭ Lydian-Aug.	C-Δ	F7+4	B7+5+9	Aø	E♭Δ+5	/G	/D
E Lydian-Aug.	C#-Δ	F#7+4	C7+5+9	B♭ø	EΔ+5	/G#	/D#
F Lydian-Aug.	D-Δ	G7+4	D♭7+5+9	Bø	FΔ+5	/A	/E
G♭ Lydian-Aug.	E♭-Δ	A♭7+4	D7+5+9	Cø	G♭Δ+5	/B♭	/F
G Lydian-Aug.	E-Δ	A7+4	E♭7+5+9	C#ø	GΔ+5	/B	/F#
A♭ Lydian-Aug.	F-Δ	B♭7+4	E7+5+9	Dø	A♭Δ+5	/C	/G
A Lydian-Aug.	F#-Δ	B7+4	F7+5+9	E♭ø	AΔ+5	/C#	/G#
B♭ Lydian-Aug.	G-Δ	C7+4	G♭7+5+9	Eø	B♭Δ+5	/D	/A
B Lydian-Aug.	A♭-Δ	D♭7+4	G7+5+9	Fø	BΔ+5	/D#	/A#
C Lydian-Aug.	A-Δ	D7+4	A♭7+5+9	F#ø	CΔ+5	/E	/B
D♭ Lydian-Aug.	B♭-Δ	E♭7+4	A7+5+9	Gø	D♭Δ+5	/F	/C
D Lydian-Aug.	B-Δ	E7+4	B♭7+5+9	G#ø	DΔ+5	/F#	/C#

APPENDIX

An Office Inventory For Jazz Education

The following inventory includes all the materials I find necessary to have near me when operating a jazz program. It is not meant to be a complete list of everything you might need to teach a jazz program, but merely an illustration. I have not listed materials used for teaching non-jazz courses. I would suggest that, should you enter the field of jazz teaching, you dig out this list, upon entering your studio for the first time, and use it as a partial check list, that you may approximate your needs. I have split the list so that you may see what the school might be expected to provide, contrasted with what you may need to provide for yourself and your students.

Personally Owned

Equipment and furnishings

baby grand piano

Rhodes piano

truck dolly

2-3 amplifiers

8 musical instruments (+pianos)

8 cords (guitar,patch,extension)

portable playback system, metronome

m.s. pens, ink, stamps,ruler,etc. typewriter

Music (on paper)

100 big band arrangements

50 small band arrangements

250 tunes (melody & changes) (files)

150 transcribed solos (files)

25 books of transcribed solos

2 Real Books (fake book)Pocket Changes

Audio-visual materials

258 slides for jazz history

School Owned

Equipment and furnishings

filing cabinet

desk

chairs

playback unit and speakers

combination slide-cassette machine

chalkboard

Music (on paper)

31 big band arrangements

8 small band arrangements

15 slides for improvisation, Coker Posters
12 transparencies for improvisation
3 sets of flashcards for improvisation
500 78 RPMs
150 general reference lps
50 play-along lps (and booklets)
41 open reel tapes
100 general reference cassettes
45 jazz history cassettes
30 cassettes (misc.) for teaching AJS, JT,
JP, JD, etc.
100 improvisation cassettes
5 jazz piano cassettes

Books
160 books on jazz (methods, history)
file folders 40 improvisation hand-outs
27 miscellaneous hand-outs
20 jazz piano hand-outs
30 jazz program administration
32 jazz theory
12 jazz history
10 AJS
30 jazz pedagogy
20 jazz arranging/composing

Miscellaneous
50 copies jazz history listening lists
(hand-outs)
50 copies jazz history slide lists (hand-outs)
manuscript paper (many sheets, many kinds)
autobiographical material

Miscellaneous
bulletins
class schedule books
miscellaneous booklets on school
policies, procedures, etc.

Proficiency Requirements For Studio Music And Jazz Majors

All Studio Music And Jazz majors are required to take proficiency examinations. The reasons for these proficiencies are: (1) to better prepare SMJ majors for a career in music; (2) to promote standards of excellence in junior and senior recitals; and (3) to insure the credibility of the SMJ degree.

The examining panel for the proficiencies consists of all members of the jazz faculty.

Dates for the proficiencies will be posted on bulletin boards. They will generally take place in the middle of each term, on a Friday. New SMJ majors (freshmen and transfer students) should take the first scheduled proficiency after their entry into the program, so that their levels may be established as early as possible, and so that each student will know what levels to attempt in his/her next proficiency. Once the levels have been determined (in the first proficiency), the students may pass up scheduled proficiencies until such time as they feel ready, so long as they achieve level 3 of each area of the proficiencies in the term preceding a scheduled Junior Recital. Students who have completed Level 3 in all areas of the proficiencies need not be further tested.

The areas of examination are:

(1) sight-reading of lines and melodies;
(2) sight-reading of chord progressions (comping), for guitarists, pianists, and vibists only;
(3) scales;
(4) arpeggios;
(5) prepared tune.

With regard to item 5 (prepared tune), each member of the jazz faculty has prepared lists of tunes from which you may select one of your choice. The lists are divided into groups of tunes that are appropriate for each of the proficiency levels (1, 2, and 3). You may obtain a copy of the tune lists from your applied instructor. For the first proficiency, you and your instructor will have to confer on the tune level to be attempted, giving it your best shot, but bearing in mind that a good performance of "Blue Bossa" (level 1, would be better than a poor performance of the fast version of "Giant Steps" (level 3).

After the first proficiency you will notified of the levels you achieved, so that you can then study the materials of the next level until such time as you feel ready to be tested. Remember that it is likely that you will score differently in different areas of the proficiency. For example, it is possible that you might achieve level 3 in tune preparation, yet fail to achieve even level 1 in melodic sight-reading.

Each jazz faculty member has the option of adding an item or two to the proficiency for their own students only. For example, the bass instructor might ask the bass students to construct bass lines on a progression that is being sight-read or the drum instructor might insist that the drummers perform in various rhythmic styles, such as swing, rock, bossa nova, etc.

In all cases, students are expected to use correct instrumental techniques, i.e. correct fingerings or slide positions, correct embouchures, good tone quality and just intonation, etc.

APPENDIX

Guidelines For Jazz Recitals

The jazz recital is intended for use by jazz majors only. Departmental policy states that the student must be enrolled for applied music lessons during the term in which the recital is to be given. Studio Music and Jazz majors are required to give a half-recital (Music 3000) near the end of their junior year and a full recital (Music 4000) near the end of their senior year. A recital should reflect all aspects of the student's consummate development, such as improvisation, composing and arranging, ensemble playing, leadership, programming, instrumental ability, versatility (stylistic and perhaps instrumental), and the ability to select and organize assisting players.

The jazz recital should be approached chiefly as a solo recital, focusing on a single player rather than as an ensemble recital (this approach might be moderated somewhat in the case of bassists and drummers, since their function as members of the rhythm section carries considerable responsibility). Under no circumstances should the recital be approached in the manner of a loosely organized jam session. Brief solos by supporting players may be included, but they must not dilute the overall effect of a solo recital.

The assisting players will generally comprise a small group (rhythm section plus optional horns), but a variety in this respect, such as unaccompanied solos, duos, trios, or even large ensemble selections, is also welcome.

Original compositions and arrangements by the student giving the recital are most appropriate, though other well-selected tunes from established jazz artists/composers are also appropriate, especially if their inclusion would promote a well-rounded program, in terms of vehicle-types and tempos. The program may include some classical literature, if the student's background and training seems to dictate that it would be appropriate.

Since all aspects of the recital will be critiqued by the jazz faculty, a copy of the adjudication form will be available upon request, to assist the student in knowing the items that will be considered in the critiques. After the recital has been given, the completed adjudication sheets will be given to the student.

The student is responsible for all mechanics of the recital. A check list is provided below to aid the student in this respect. Items which do not show in the list below, but for which the student is nevertheless responsible include selection and organization of assisting personnel, scheduling and conducting rehearsals, staging, lighting, sound system, recording (optional), and seeing that all performers are in formal attire (tuxedo) for the recital.

Recital Check List

- ☐ Select and reserve a date and time for the recital by conferring with the Auditorium Supervisor (do this early, as the calendar dates are scarce).
- ☐ Notify all members of the jazz faculty of the date as soon as you know it.
- ☐ Be sure that you are enrolled for applied lessons in the term of your recital.
- ☐ Submit a proposed program to the jazz faculty for approval.
- ☐ Schedule a recital hearing, to take place no later than two weeks prior to the recital. Notify all members of the jazz faculty of the date, time, and place of the hearing. Bear in mind that the hearing is not a rehearsal, but a presentation of the final level of performance. The recital may be cancelled by the jazz faculty, at this point, if the hearing is weak.
- ☐ If the hearing is successful, submit the program to the music school office, allowing two weeks for printing.

- ☐ Submit another copy of the program, plus a brief press release, to the Publicity Director, who will assist you in seeing that the recital is mentioned in the school paper and perhaps other newspapers.
- ☐ Have some sort of poster made and get them distributed and posted, on campus and in the windows of local businesses, especially music shops, record stores, and lounges.
- ☐ Call and write to friends and relatives who might be able to attend.
- ☐ Contact local radio stations and request having your recital mentioned in the afternoon jazz program and in the morning Community Arts Calendar. Also try to get an announcement on the Community Events Calendars of at least one of the local television stations.
- ☐ When the programs return from the printer, post copies in the music building a few days before the recital.
- ☐ Be sure to schedule at least a couple of rehearsals after the hearing, as the jazz faculty will probably suggest a few improvements at the hearing. If you plan to have a dress rehearsal in the auditorium, be sure to reserve a time. Consider a soundcheck, and let the Auditorium Supervisor know if you want him to tape the recital (he may ask you to purchase and bring your own tape).
- ☐ Take care of all equipment needs, such as sound system, electric piano, synthesizer, staging needs, etc., well in advance, so that you can concentrate on the music during the last week before the recital.
- ☐ If you want ushers, the music fraternity and sorority are often willing to provide you with same.
- ☐ Be sure to consider stage deportment, for yourself and for the group. Learn to bow gracefully (observe others, if you need help

with this). Decide how the group will enter and exit the stage, and whether they will precede or follow you on and off stage. Be ready to handle a curtain call gracefully, if needed. Decide whether or not you will say anything to the audience anytime during the program, and what you will say, if anything.

- ☐ Consider whether or not you will need to enlist the help of friends to move equipment during the performance. If so, request that they be attractively dressed for the task.
- ☐ Be sure that the programs are in the lobby prior to the recital, accessible to the audience as they arrive.

If you want the Studio Music and Jazz Majors (and others) to attend *your* recital, then you should attend *theirs* (you should attend, anyway).

Jr./Sr. Recital by: ______________________ Date: __________

Performance	Organization
Instrumental Techniques *(tone, intonation, etc.)*	**Attire / Stage Deportment**
Interpretation *(rhythm, time-feeling, phrasing, spirit, drive, etc.)*	**Stage / Lighting**
Tonal Materials *(changes / scales)*	**Sound System**
Improvisation	**Printed Program** *(order, inclusion)*
Original Composition	**Leadership**
Ensemble	**Promotion /Advertising**

Comments:

Suggested Grade: ______________ Signed: ____________________

Mayday.... From the Locker Room at Half-Time

Jazz education has arrived at an exceedingly crucial stage of development. Jazz programs are proliferating at an amazing rate! The reasons are obvious. I think ... increased enrollment and prestige for the sagging music departments, increased attendance for public performances, cheap labor, and the 'quick fix' syndrome. Furthermore, jazz music has developed into a very complex art/skill most worthy of dedicated study, the programs which teach the music have been long overdue (so much for our wisdom and foresight, eh), hence many have been waiting for that event to take place, and quickly fill the programs as fast as they can be installed. You know all this, right? That's the good news. The bad news is that we are not really ready to handle the good news. The inanimate items are relatively ready (books, records, tune books, solo transcriptions, etc.), but are we ready?

The basic problem is that the students are already in place, waiting to be enlightened, whereas we have far too few jazz educators to handle them, and only a handful of fully-qualified ones at that. We certainly appreciate the interest and willingness to participate, with respect to 'crossover' teachers (classically-trained colleagues already entrenched at the school), graduate assistants, and part-time help from the outside (local professionals), but this can only be a temporary stop-gap measure, in most cases, unless the helpers become fully-dedicated to the project. We have waited far too long to begin training quality jazz educators, yet we are already confronted with the need to supply the demand. To be accurate, we have had the problem since about 1970 (15 years!) generally speaking, and schools which had jazz programs in the early years (1947-1969) were hard-pressed to find anyone who could teach some jazz, and have been facing the problem for a much longer time.

I have always felt blessed to have come into the world when I did. The timing permitted me to hear and know someone like Sidney

Bechet, from very early jazz, but also hear and know someone like Randy Brecker today. My father was a swing era tenor saxophonist, playing when jazz was an immensely popular music, providing me with an inspiring bombardment of the jazz of that time (jazz was on record, in movie theatres, live on radio at prime time, plus I heard many of my father's gigs, broadcasts, rehearsals, sessions, and practice). I was an impressionable teenager, studying jazz, when the bebop era began, the first (and perhaps most significant) period in which it was clearly established (by example) that jazz music would no longer be all play and no work.

Players like Bird and Diz made it obvious that instrumental virtuosity and style are merely the tip of the iceberg. Their choice of notes and phrases went beyond ear-playing and into a whole new realm of needs (improvisational theory and practice) for young players like yours truly. We were advised that if we would study traditional music theory, composition, history, applied lessons, and ensembles, that all would be revealed that would serve our purposes for learning jazz. The advice was well-meant and good, but they were wrong, nonetheless, and we had nowhere to turn. But as young adults our opportunity was to begin to correct the problem. A young jazz educator today might have trouble comprehending the scope of such an opportunity. He (or she, in each reference) would have to imagine a world without books, methods, play-alongs, video tapes, computers, course outlines, curriculum models, even usable arrangements, etc. Then he'd have to add to that that he, like us, had been largely self-taught (asking questions, watching, transcribing, experimenting, using trial and error, and the like). That in itself was good timing, as my generation is the last that can remember what it was like to be selftaught and compare that, pros and cons, with the way jazz is studied today.

But the greatest blessing, for those of us who were and still are involved with the developement of jazz methods, courses, and curricula, is that we had the opportunity to pioneer the educational training of young jazz musicians; that is, with no models to adhere to, we could try to avoid some of the pitfalls we remembered from our non-jazz training. We saw our fellow students being carefully trained for a profession that doesn't really exist (Have you tried to place one of your prize students in a symphony orchestra lately?) We heard young people being advised that they should go into music education if they see that they don't love music enough to become a performer. These are only two of many pitfalls, and I would hope that we can avoid them by making sure that we are both artistic and practical in our approach to coaching young players for the world of music that does exist (all styles), and by making it clear that they must become (and remain!) good performers, as good as they can be, if they expect to become good jazz educators.

Your Responsibility To Integrity

I sometimes ask my students questions like "how badly do you want to reach your fullest potential?", "Do you think that your peer group in other areas of the world are working no harder than you are?", "Do you think that Trane and other giants worked no harder than you do?", or "How much do you love jazz?" Mostly I feel that young players sometimes need to come to grips with the ardours and complexities of studying jazz, particularly in the areas of instrumental and improvisational study. It takes many years (more than four, for sure) to learn to play an instrument well enough to meet the needs of playing jazz and we need a lifetime (at least) to really develop to our fullest potential in improvisation! We can 'learn our changes' in a relatively short span of, say, a year or less, but we're not making much music at that stage. There are many long, sometimes continuous, disciplines to master (or die trying), like learning and playing transcribed solos, listening to records, collecting and transposing licks, working on bright tempos, improvising in all keys with equal facility, learning several thousand melodies and progressions, consuming books of patterns, working for an even ability on all types (vehicles) of tunes, etc. The list is awesome, certainly more than can be accomplished in four years at the practice rate of 1-2 hours per day. Jazz programs offer information, feedback, hints on efficiency, and help with organizing your practice habits, but the real work must then begin, as no one can practice for you.

The list may be awesome, but it is the responsibility of all jazz educators to become and remain perpetually involved with the practice, performance, and demonstration of these items and more, on their instruments. We cannot simply conduct and /or lecture about the music. Would you teach conducting or teach people how to lecture without conducting or lecturing yourself? Of course not. Nor would you expect to obtain a maximum result in an improvisation class, for example, if you cannot or won't play for them, nor will you continue to learn. If you feel stylistically dated and therefore reluctant to perform in class with your modern and/or more-gifted students, then do something about it. Listen to their records, learn to play the transcribed solos of more modern players, be patient with the slowness of change, practice with play-alongs of more modern tunes, and look for opportunities to practice and perform with younger players.

Remember too, that your gifted young players have problems, also. They lack your years of hearing and playing experiences, and much of what you learned they may never learn, resulting in young players with little depth, stylistically, and less spontaneity and originality than you might think. They, too, get locked in if they're not careful. For example, a young tenor player may adopt someone like Michael Brecker as a musical guru, to the exclusion of all other tenor players, and learn all of Mike's best licks and emulate his sound. This is natural, but it is an immature stage. The model (Brecker) is great, perhaps, our greatest living jazz saxophonist, and he's my present favorite, but I view my influence by him as one in a long chain of influences over the years, and I still emulate, in ways, the playing of other present-day players.

The student who decides to become a Brecker clone has taken an important step and may even enjoy early professional success, but must eventually spread out, stylistically...or risk sounding shallow. Ten years down the line he may be still lacking personal identity; locked into the music of his youth. (Mike will probably have changed much of his style by then, to accommodate his own urge for change.) So, as an educator, unless you're interested in the whole idiom of jazz and its incessant changes, you will shortchange yourself, become stagnated, and become a less-effective teacher/performer.

Be A Working Model

In closing I should like to offer a few thoughts about teaching a jazz program, with respect to the necessary effort. Keep up your horn. Don't get stylistically locked in. Stay abreast of new developments in methods, courses, curricula, trends, etc. Gird yourself for the effort - teaching jazz is a very demanding effort, physically, mentally, and emotionally (wear your jeans to work!) If you don't find it so, then you're not doing it very well. Don't be afraid to experiment with the curriculum. Always look for better ways to handle courses and ensembles, reassessing your effort constantly. Live the example you want for your students. Pray that your better students learn to challenge your authority and level of performance (in a noncombative way). It is an important sign of their growing maturity, and unless they assert themselves, they can never achieve the needed level of conviction. Don't expect praise or gratitude from your students; it may be all give! Get healthy and stay that way. Never give up on any student who is making the effort, as we all have different rates of learning and assimilation. One student may become a good player in two years, another student may become a great player in twelve years. Which was the better student, and how did you regard and handle each?

Think of yourself as perpetual student. Attend the special clinics given by Jamey Aebersold for educators only, and audit or attend his camps. Share ideas with other teachers with similar challenges and goals in combined strength. Music is the whole .. we are its parts, not the other way around. Make sure your students have every opportunity to love jazz music. Delight them with your dedication to the music and your total commitment to their learning needs.